Building Real-Life
READING SKILLS

Cindy Harris

New York • Toronto • London • Auckland • Sydney
Mexico City • New Delhi • Hong Kong • Buenos Aires

Teaching *Resources*

To my children—the inspiration behind this book—and to my husband—for his conviction that I could make it a reality.
—Cindy Harris

Scholastic Inc. grants teachers permission to photocopy the reproducible pages from this book for classroom use. No other part of this publication may be reproduced in whole or in part, or stored in a retrieval system, or transmitted in any form or by any means, electronic, mechanical, photocopying, recording, or otherwise, without written permission of the publisher. For information regarding permission, write to Scholastic Inc., 557 Broadway, New York, NY 10012.

Editor: Sarah Longhi
Production editing: Eileen Judge
Cover design: Holly Grundon
Interior design: Kelli Thompson
Illustrations: Kelli Thompson and Andrew Jenkins

ISBN-13: 978-0-439-92321-7
ISBN-10: 0-439-92321-2

5 6 7 8 9 10   40   15 14 13 12

Contents

Introduction

So often students ask, "What's the point of learning *this*?" or "Why do I need to know *this*?" You won't hear comments like that using this book, because the lessons target *real* texts whose meanings have *real* value in the daily lives of our students—both in and out of school. Building real-life reading skills helps students gain a greater understanding of the world around them and the confidence to participate more fully in it.

What Is Real-Life Reading?

Real-life reading is the reading we encounter every day in our homes, stores, schools, communities, and the world at large. The real-life texts we encounter include advertisements, labels, schedules, forms, bulletins, and menus to name a few. Children feel empowered when they're able to read and interpret real-life information. In the information age, this is an essential skill.

How to Use This Book

The self-inclusive lessons in this book are geared toward third, fourth, and fifth graders. They can be used in any order and as frequently as you desire to fit your curriculum. You may adapt the lessons for whole-class or small-group work.

Teaching Routine

Each real-life reading lesson is three pages long and follows the same format:

First Page: *Teaching Guide*

Second Page: *Let's Read Together*—a reproducible introductory activity that you and students use together to learn about the example of real-life reading

Third Page: *Now It's Your Turn*—a reproducible practice page featuring a similar type of real-life reading so that students can apply their new knowledge

A synopsis of each page follows.

Real-life reading supports

- reading comprehension skills
- standardized testing skills
- vocabulary skills
- independent decision-making

First Page: Teaching Guide

The lesson begins with a *Real-Life Scenario* read-aloud—a brief, fictional scenario that engages students by giving them a context for understanding why this type of real-life reading is important. The scenario is about a boy or girl in a situation that necessitates real-life reading. It sets the stage for the lesson.

What's at Stake sums up why it's important for the child featured in the scenario to be able to read and analyze this text. It states the consequences or the benefits of having real-life reading skills.

The **Teach** section is a five-step routine for teaching students about the real-life reading text that appears on the *Let's Read Together* page:

Step 1: Set the stage by reading the *Real-Life Scenario* and *What's at Stake* sections to students. Many lessons also offer discussion topics here to help build background.

Step 2: Introduce students to the vocabulary in the *Words to Know* box. Present the real-life literacy text to students. Point out key concepts.

Step 3: Ask the *Guided Questions* to help students analyze the real-life reading text. (An answer key is provided at the back of the book.) Have students complete the *Vocabulary Quick Check*.

Step 4: Share the *Did You Know?* trivia with students. Discuss the *Think About It!* question and the *Be Smart!* box from the *Let's Read Together* page. (Note: Some lessons do not have all these features.)

Step 5: Send off students to complete the *Now It's Your Turn* activity.

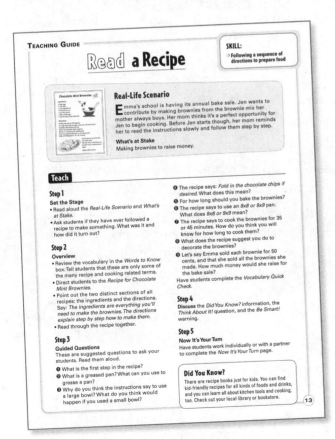

Teaching Guide for *Read a Recipe* lesson (page 13)

***Chocolate Mint Brownies*: One of two real-life texts included in the lesson (page 14)**

Let's Read Together reproducible
page for guided practice (page 14)

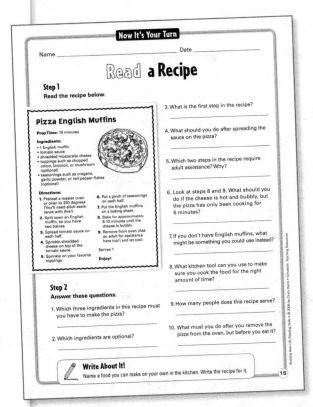

Now It's Your Turn reproducible page
for independent practice (page 15)

Second Page: *Let's Read Together*

This reproducible page features a model real-life text. Students use this page as you explain the features of the text and ask them questions. To enhance the teaching and learning experience, this page of each lesson also includes:

• A *Words to Know* box with essential vocabulary for real-life reading

• A *Vocabulary Quick Check* activity box to reinforce vocabulary

• A *Think About It!* question to extend students' thinking and initiate questions/discussions

• *Be Smart!* knowledge and trivia features

Third Page: *Now It's Your Turn*

This part of the lesson is a practice page for students. This reproducible activity gives them the opportunity to apply their new knowledge. Students can complete this page independently, with a partner, in a small group, or as homework. (Encourage them to refer back to the *Let's Read Together* page as necessary.) This practice page includes:

• A second model of a real-life text to read and think about

• Questions about the text that require students to use their newly acquired skills

• A *Write About It!* task that prompts students to further apply their learning in a new scenario and allows you to assess how well students have learned the target skills

Tip!

These reproducible pages offer students space to write short responses to the questions. If you prefer for students to answer in complete sentences, consider having them use the back of the page or a notebook page.

Read a Sign for Store Hours

Store Hours			
Mon.	9:30 am	to	7:00 pm
Tues.	9:30 am	to	9:30 pm
Wed.	9:30 am	to	7:00 pm
Thur.	10:00 am	to	9:00 pm
Fri.	9:30 am	to	10:00 pm
Sat.	11:00 am	to	5:00 pm
Sun.	Closed	to	

Real-Life Scenario

Latoya can't believe it. After waiting all week to go to the bookstore, she and her father arrived on Sunday to find a sign on the door that said "CLOSED." Her father promised they would come back again during the week. But, they need to find out what night the store is open late so that they can go after her father gets home from work. Latoya looks at the sign, wondering just how many days she'll have to wait.

What's at Stake

Knowing when to come back to the bookstore so that Latoya can buy the books she wants.

Teach

Step 1
Set the Stage
- Read aloud the *Real-Life Scenario* and *What's at Stake* above.
- Ask students where stores usually post signs to say when they are open for business. (*on the door or storefront window*)

Step 2
Overview
- Distribute copies of the *Let's Read Together* page.
- Review the meanings of *a.m.* and *p.m.* in the *Abbreviations to Know* box.
- Read through the sign with students. Model how to look for information on this sign. For example, say: *Each day and its store hours appear in a separate row. On Tuesday, for instance, I see that the store is open from 9:30 in the morning until 9:30 at night.*

Step 3
Ask Guided Questions
These are suggested questions to ask your students. Read them aloud.

❶ If Latoya's father can't bring her to the store until at least 8:00 in the evening, what day is the soonest day that they can go back to the store?

❷ Which day of the week has the longest store hours?

❸ Which day has the shortest hours?

❹ On most days of the week, what time does the store open?

❺ What two days of the week have identical hours?

Have students complete the *Vocabulary Quick Check.*

Step 4
Discuss the *Think About It!* question and the *Be Smart!* question regarding store hours.

Step 5
Now It's Your Turn
Distribute copies of the *Now It's Your Turn* reproducible. Have students work individually or with a partner to complete the activity.

Name _____ Date _____

Read a Sign for Store Hours

Store Hours

Mon.	9:30 am	to	7:00 pm
Tues.	9:30 am	to	9:30 pm
Wed.	9:30 am	to	7:00 pm
Thur.	10:00 am	to	9:00 pm
Fri.	9:30 am	to	10:00 pm
Sat.	11:00 am	to	5:00 pm
Sun.	Closed	to	

Abbreviations to Know

a.m. or AM is an abbreviation for the times of the day between midnight and noon (origin from Latin *ante meridiem*, meaning "before midday" or "before noon")

p.m. or PM is an abbreviation for the times of day between noon and midnight (origin from Latin *post meridiem*, meaning "after midday" or "after noon")

Think About It!

Many stores have longer hours on Fridays and Saturdays. Why do you think stores stay open later on these days?

Be Smart!

You can usually count on a store to be open during the hours their sign says they'll be open. But most stores are closed on holidays. This information might not be posted on the sign. Can you think of a holiday when a store will likely be closed?

Vocabulary Quick Check

Is it a.m. or p.m.?

1. Is 2:30 in the afternoon a.m. or p.m.?

    _____.

2. Is 11:59 at night a.m. or p.m.?

    _____.

3. Is 12 noon a.m. or p.m.?

    _____.

Building Real-Life Reading Skills • © 2009 by Cindy Harris • Scholastic Teaching Resources

Name _____ Date _____

Read a Sign for Store Hours

Step 1 Look at the store hours information below that was posted online.

Caravelle Electronics

Allwood Street Location	Colfax Avenue Location
1430 Allwood Street	256 Colfax Avenue
Denver, CO 80202	Denver, CO 80206
303-555-0000	303-800-2229
electronics@caravelle.com	electronics@caravelle.com

Store Hours		Store Hours	
Monday	7:00 a.m. to 9:00 p.m.	Monday	9:00 a.m. to 10:00 p.m.
Tuesday	7:00 a.m. to 9:00 p.m.	Tuesday	9:00 a.m. to 10:00 p.m.
Wednesday	7:00 a.m. to 9:00 p.m.	Wednesday	9:00 a.m. to 10:00 p.m.
Thursday	7:00 a.m. to 9:00 p.m.	Thursday	9:00 a.m. to 10:00 p.m.
Friday	7:00 a.m. to 11:00 p.m.	Friday	9:00 a.m. to 11:00 p.m.
Saturday	9:00 a.m. to 11:00 p.m.	Saturday	9:00 a.m. to 11:00 p.m.
Sunday	10:00 a.m. to 6:00 p.m.	Sunday	9:00 a.m. to 6:00 p.m.

Step 2

Answer these questions.

1. How late can you shop at this store on a Saturday night?

_____

2. Is either location open at 8:00 a.m.? If so, which one?

_____

3. Is either location open until midnight? If so, which one?

_____

4. Which location is opened the latest on Mondays and Tuesdays?

_____

5. Which location opens the earliest?

_____

6. Which location stays open the latest on most nights?

_____

7. Which location has longer hours on Sundays?

_____

8. Suppose you wanted to ask the store if an item is in stock before you go to the store. What are two ways you could contact the store to ask your question?

_____

_____

Write About It!

Imagine that you own a store. Your store is open every day from 10 a.m. until 5 p.m. It is closed on Sundays. On a separate sheet of paper, make a sign that displays your store hours.

Building Real-Life Reading Skills • © 2009 by Cindy Harris • Scholastic Teaching Resources

Read an Invitation & Directions

Shhh... It's a Surprise!!!

For: Miguel's 10th Birthday

Date: Friday, May 3rd

Time: Please arrive at 4:30! Don't be late!

Place: Miguel's Home
65 Ridge Road

R.S.V.P. Regrets Only by email:
m.family@martinez.com

Directions from school to our home:
Head out of the school driveway and make a right on Oak Street.
Walk two blocks.
Turn left onto Ridge Road.
Go to the end of Ridge Road.
Our home is at the intersection of Ridge Road and Pine Lane.
It's a blue corner house. #65

Real-Life Scenario

When Carlos came home after school, he found an invitation for Miguel's upcoming surprise birthday party. The invitation made a big point of asking classmates to get to the party in time to surprise Miguel. Although Carlos has never been to Miguel's house before, the invitation gave clear walking directions to Miguel's house from school. Carlos is sure that he and his friends will figure out the directions together.

What's at Stake
Getting to the party and not ruining the surprise for Miguel.

Teach

Step 1
Set the Stage
• Read aloud the *Real-Life Scenario* and *What's at Stake*.

Step 2
Overview
• Review the vocabulary in the *Words to Know* box.
• Read the *Invitation & Directions* together.
• Ask students to point out the distinct pieces of information that an invitation includes such as the *date*, *time*, *place*, *RSVP instructions*, etc.
• Show students the directions at the bottom of the invitation. Point out that the directions explain exactly how to get to the party. Tell students that directions are sometimes printed on a separate paper insert.

Step 3
Guided Questions
These are suggested questions to ask your students. Read them aloud.

❶ How old will Miguel be?
❷ What is the date and time of the party?
❸ Where will the party be taking place?

❹ Does the Martinez family want everyone to RSVP? How do you know?
❺ If Carlos can't go to the party, what should he do to let Miguel's family know?
❻ How does Carlos get to Oak Street from school?
❼ What should Carlos do once he is on Oak Street?
❽ What additional information is given to help people find the house?

Have students complete the *Vocabulary Quick Check*.

Step 4
Discuss the *Did You Know?* trivia about birthday parties, the *Think About It!* question, and the *Be Smart!* White House greeting card offer.

Step 5
Now It's Your Turn
Have students work individually or with a partner to complete the *Now It's Your Turn* page.

Did You Know?
The earliest birthday parties began because people feared that evil spirits would visit them on their birthday each year. For protection, they would gather around their family and friends. Today, birthday parties are held for fun!

Name _____ Date _____

Read an Invitation & Directions

Shhh... It's a Surprise!!!

★ • ★ • ★ • ★ • ★ • ★ • ★ • ★ • ★ • ★

For: Miguel's 10th Birthday

Date: Friday, May 3rd

Time: Please arrive at 4:30! Don't be late!

Place: Miguel's Home
            65 Ridge Road

R.S.V.P. Regrets Only by email:
            m.family@martinez.com

- -

Directions from school to our home:

Head out of the school driveway and make
a right on Oak Street.

Walk two blocks.

Turn left onto Ridge Road.

Go to the end of Ridge Road.

Our home is at the intersection of Ridge
Road and Pine Lane.

It's a blue corner house. #65

Words to Know

RSVP—abbreviation for the French phrase meaning "please reply"

regrets only—respond only if you're not able to attend

intersection—a point at which two roads meet

head—go

block—one street

Vocabulary Quick Check
Synonyms

1. A synonym for *road* is

_____.

2. A synonym for *travel* is

_____.

3. A synonym for *respond* is

_____.

 ## Think About It!

*Why do you think people would send an invitation
that says:* RSVP Regrets Only instead of RSVP?

Be Smart!

Would you like to surprise a special person who is 80 years old or older on his or her birthday?
The White House will send a special birthday card to that person if you write to them at:

White House Greeting Officer
OEOB, Room 39
Washington, DC 20500

Include the person's name, address, age, and birth date.

Name _____ Date _____

Read an Invitation & Directions

Step 1
Read the Boy Scout invitation and walking directions below.

Boy Scout—Troop 12

Barbecue Cookout
At Memorial Park

Tuesday, June 5th
(after school)

4:00–6:00 p.m.

Fee **$5**

RSVP by email to
Scout Master John Conner
conner@troop12boyscouts.org

Directions from school to Memorial Park

Make a right on Campbell Road.
Head north. Walk two and a half blocks.
Make a left on Independence Way.
At the next intersection, turn left onto Memorial Drive.
Our troop will meet by Memorial Statue.

 Write About It!

Pick one:

Choice 1. Imagine that you are having a party. Write directions for your friends to let them know how to get from school to your home.

Choice 2. Imagine you're having a birthday party. Write an invitation that tells your friends everything they need to know to come to your party.

Step 2
Answer these questions.

1. Where and when is the cookout?

   _____

   _____

2. How many hours will the cookout last?

   _____

3. What does the cookout cost? _____

4. Whom should the scouts notify to say whether or not they can attend?

   _____

5. How should they notify him?

   _____

6. What is the starting point for the directions for getting to Memorial Park?

   _____

7. In what direction should the scouts head when they are on Campbell Road?

   _____

8. What should scouts do when they get to Independence Way?

   _____

9. From the directions, can you figure out the name of the road that leads into the park?

   _____

10. At what landmark will the troop meet? What time will they meet there?

   _____

Building Real-Life Reading Skills • © 2009 by Cindy Harris • Scholastic Teaching Resources

Read a Recipe

SKILL:
○ Following a sequence of directions to prepare food

Real-Life Scenario

Emma's school is having its annual bake sale. Jen wants to contribute by making brownies from the brownie mix her mother always buys. Her mom thinks it's a perfect opportunity for Jen to begin cooking. Before Jen starts though, her mom reminds her to read the instructions slowly and follow them step by step.

What's at Stake
Making brownies to raise money.

Teach

Step 1

Set the Stage
- Read aloud the *Real-Life Scenario* and *What's at Stake*.
- Ask students if they have ever followed a recipe to make something. What was it and how did it turn out?

Step 2

Overview
- Review the vocabulary in the *Words to Know* box. Tell students that these are only some of the many recipe and cooking related terms.
- Direct students to the *Recipe for Chocolate Mint Brownies*.
- Point out the two distinct sections of all recipes: the ingredients and the directions. Say: *The ingredients are everything you'll need to make the brownies. The directions explain step by step how to make them.*
- Read through the recipe together.

Step 3

Guided Questions
These are suggested questions to ask your students. Read them aloud.

❶ What is the first step in the recipe?
❷ What is a greased pan? What can you use to grease a pan?
❸ Why do you think the instructions say to use a large bowl? What do you think would happen if you used a small bowl?

❹ The recipe says: *Fold in the chocolate chips if desired.* What does this mean?
❺ For how long should you bake the brownies?
❻ The recipe says to use an *8x8 or 9x9* pan. What does *8x8 or 9x9* mean?
❼ The recipe says to cook the brownies for 35 or 45 minutes. How do you think you will know for how long to cook them?
❽ What does the recipe suggest you do to decorate the brownies?
❾ Let's say Emma sold each brownie for 50 cents, and that she sold all the brownies she made. How much money would she raise for the bake sale?

Have students complete the *Vocabulary Quick Check*.

Step 4

Discuss the *Did You Know?* information, the *Think About It!* question, and the *Be Smart!* warning.

Step 5

Now It's Your Turn
Have students work individually or with a partner to complete the *Now It's Your Turn* page.

Did You Know?

There are recipe books just for kids. You can find kid-friendly recipes for all kinds of foods and drinks, and you can learn all about kitchen tools and cooking, too. Check out your local library or bookstore.

Name _____ Date _____

Read a Recipe

Chocolate Mint Brownies

Ingredients:

2 large eggs
¼ cup water
½ cup vegetable oil
1 box brownie mix
1 tsp. mint extract
1 tbsp. vanilla sugar
1 cup chocolate chips (optional)

Directions:

Preheat the oven to 350 degrees.
In a large bowl, mix the eggs, water, oil, and mint extract.
Combine with the brownie mix.
Fold in the chocolate chips if desired.
Stir for 1-2 minutes until well blended.
Pour into a greased 8x8 pan or 9x9 square pan.
Bake at 350 degrees for 35–45 minutes.

Cool in pan or on wire rack.
Cut when cool.
Garnish with a strawberry or sprinkle with confectioners' sugar.

Makes 20 brownies.

Words to Know

optional—not necessary, may be left out

fold—mix gently

extract—a concentrated form of something used for flavoring

blend—to mix or stir two or more ingredients together until smooth

garnish—decorate

pinch—a small amount that you can hold between your thumb and forefinger

preheat—heat ahead of time

prep time—time it takes to prepare everything before eating it or cooking it

shredded—cut into very thin strips

season—to flavor

Vocabulary Quick Check

**These bold words have multiple meanings.
In cooking terms however,**

1. **season** means   a. a time of year   b. to flavor

2. **fold** means   a. lightly mix together   b. to bend in half

3. a **pinch** means   a. a squeeze   b. a tiny bit

 ## Think About It!

What do you think would happen if you didn't cook the brownies long enough? What would happen if you cooked them too long?

Be Smart!

Ovens and stoves stay hot for quite a long time after they are shut off. Never take out food from a hot oven without wearing oven mitts.

Building Real-Life Reading Skills • © 2009 by Cindy Harris • Scholastic Teaching Resources

Name _____ Date _____

Read a Recipe

Step 1
Read the recipe below.

Pizza English Muffins

Prep Time: 10 minutes

Ingredients:
- 1 English muffin
- tomato sauce
- shredded mozzarella cheese
- toppings such as chopped onion, broccoli, or mushroom (optional)
- seasonings such as oregano, garlic powder, or red pepper flakes (optional)

Directions:

1. Preheat a toaster oven or oven to 250 degrees (You'll need adult assistance with this!)
2. Split open an English muffin, so you have two halves.
3. Spread tomato sauce on each half.
4. Sprinkle shredded cheese on top of the tomato sauce.
5. Sprinkle on your favorite toppings.
6. Put a pinch of seasonings on each half.
7. Put the English muffins on a baking sheet.
8. Bake for approximately 8-10 minutes until the cheese is bubbly.
9. Remove from oven (Ask an adult for assistance here too!) and let cool.

Serves 1

Enjoy!

Step 2
Answer these questions.

1. Which three ingredients in this recipe must you have to make the pizza?

    _____

2. Which ingredients are optional?

    _____

3. What is the first step in the recipe?

    _____

4. What should you do after spreading the sauce on the pizza?

    _____

5. Which two steps in the recipe require adult assistance? Why?

    _____

6. Look at steps 8 and 9. What should you do if the cheese is hot and bubbly, but the pizza has only been cooking for 6 minutes?

    _____

7. If you don't have English muffins, what might be something you could use instead?

    _____

8. What kitchen tool can you use to make sure you cook the food for the right amount of time?

    _____

9. How many people does this recipe serve?

    _____

10. What must you do after you remove the pizza from the oven, but before you eat it?

    _____

 Write About It!
Name a food you can make on your own in the kitchen. Write the recipe for it.

Read a Check

SKILLS:
- ○ Understanding the function and key elements of a check
- ○ Writing a check

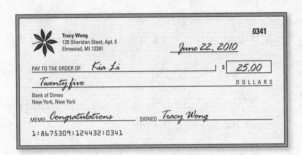

Real-Life Scenario

Kia just graduated from fifth grade and is celebrating her elementary school graduation. Several of her relatives gave her checks for a graduation gift. Kia is excited, but isn't quite sure how to figure out how much each check is worth. No one ever gave her a check before.

What's at Stake

Figuring out how much money she has received for graduation.

Teach

Step 1

Set the Stage

- Read aloud the *Real-Life Scenario* and *What's at Stake*.
- Ask students if they know what a "check" is. Discuss with students why people may prefer to use a check instead of cash.

Step 2

Overview

- Review the vocabulary in the *Words to Know* box.
- Direct students to the *Check*.
- Point out each of the call-outs to explain what each line of the check is for.
- **TIP** You may want to check out the website www.moneyinstructor.com. It offers resources for teachers such as lesson plans and worksheets to help children learn about money.

Step 3

Guided Questions

These are suggested questions to ask your students. Read them aloud.

❶ How much money is this check for? Which two places can you look to figure out the amount of money that the check is for?

❷ Which two places can you find the name of the person who is writing the check?

❸ Which line of the check is for writing a short note? What does this note say?

❹ What is the date on this check?

❺ Which line is for the name of the person that the check is made out to?

Have students complete the *Vocabulary Quick Check*.

Step 4

Discuss the *Did You Know?* item, the *Think About It!* question, and the *Be Smart!* information about checks made out to "Cash."

Step 5

Now It's Your Turn

Have students work individually or with a partner to complete the *Now It's Your Turn* page.

Did You Know?

A check is an order. It orders a bank to pay a specific amount of money to the person whom the check is made out to. Only that person whose name is on the check can cash the check.

Name _____ Date _____

Read a Check

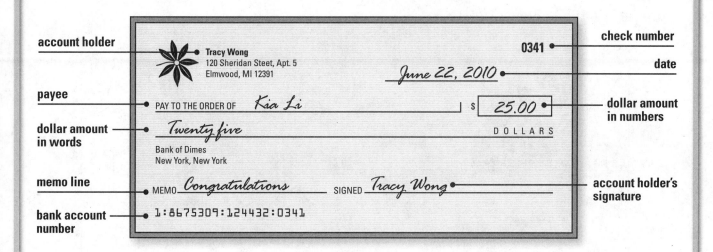

account holder — Tracy Wong
120 Sheridan Steet, Apt. 5
Elmwood, MI 12391

check number — 0341

date — *June 22, 2010*

payee — PAY TO THE ORDER OF *Kia Li* $ *25.00*

dollar amount in numbers

dollar amount in words — *Twenty five* DOLLARS

Bank of Dimes
New York, New York

memo line — MEMO *Congratulations* SIGNED *Tracy Wong*

account holder's signature

bank account number — 1:8675309:124432:0341

Words to Know

checkbook—a book of blank checks

endorse—sign your name on the back of a check that is written to you

memo line—line where the person writing the check can put a note

payee—the person to whom the check is written

payor—the person who writes the check

signature—a person's name written in script or in a special way

Vocabulary Quick Check

Complete the sentence with a word from the box.

1. If you sign your name on the back of a check you _____ it.

2. The person who writes the check to another person is the _____.

3. The place to write a short note on a check is called the _____.

Be Smart! _____

Let's say your grandparents give you a check. Instead of writing *your name* on it, they write *Cash*. If a check is made out to *Cash*, this means that check is just like having cash. Anyone who takes the check to the bank can cash it in for money. So, if you ever get a check made out to *Cash*, hold onto it tightly! It's just like having dollar bills in your hand.

 Think About It!

Why do you think a person has to sign a check?

Name _____ Date _____

Read a Check

Step 1

Look at the blank check below.

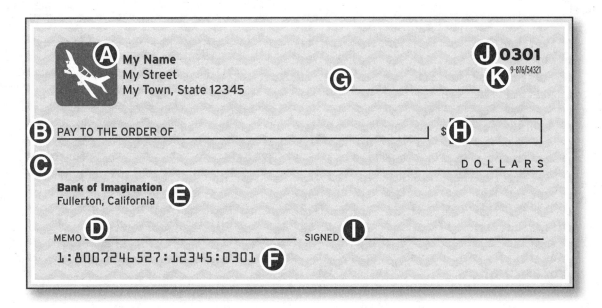

Step 2

Answer these questions.

1. On which line would you write the phrase "Sixty-five dollars"?

_____

2. On which line does the "date" of the check go?

_____

3. Which line is used for the "signature" of the person writing the check?

_____

4. Which line might be used to write a "note"?

_____

5. Where would the numbers "65.00" go?

_____

6. Which line is used to write the payee's name?

_____

7. Next to which letter can you find the name and address of the person who is writing the check?

_____

8. Which letter is next to the name of the bank?

_____

Write About It!

Imagine that this check is from your own checkbook. You owe your friend Ethan Jones $15 for some books that he bought for you. Write Ethan a check. Fill in all the information.

18

Read a Restaurant Menu

SKILLS:
- Reading a menu
- Recognizing/understanding borrowed words

Dinner Menu
(served from 4PM)

Hors d'Oeuvres
Escargot (snails) in garlic butter
Quiche with vegetables and cheese
Shrimp Cocktail

Soups
French Onion Soup
Soup du Jour

Entrées
Fried Chicken with mashed potatoes
Rack of Lamb with rice
Grilled Salmon with potatoes
Steak with fries
Stuffed Portobello Mushrooms
All the above served with salad and house dressing
Salad Nicoise with fresh tuna

A la carte
French fries   wild rice
mashed potatoes   grilled vegetables

Desserts
Sorbet • Chocolate Mousse • Fondue • Seasonal Fruits

18% Gratuity Added to the Bill

Real-Life Scenario

It's Brendan's birthday. Grandpa George and Grandma Dorothy are taking him to a fancy restaurant. Brendan knows the menu at *Burger Delight* by heart, but the menu at this restaurant has him stumped. Half the menu seems like it's written in a foreign language. Brendan wonders how he is supposed to enjoy his birthday dinner when he can't even figure out what to order.

What's at Stake
Ordering something he likes for his birthday dinner.

Teach

Step 1
Set the Stage
- Read aloud the *Real-Life Scenario* and *What's at Stake*.
- Generate a discussion about students' favorite restaurants and what they like to order there. You may want to discuss the differences between a fast-food restaurant and a regular restaurant.

Step 2
Overview
- Review the vocabulary in the *Words to Know box*.
- Read through the *Dinner Menu* with students.
- Point out how the menu is organized in sections: *Hors D'oeuvres, Soups, Entrées*, etc.

Step 3
Guided Questions
These are suggested questions to ask your students. Read them aloud.

❶ What kind of cuisine is served at this restaurant?

❷ At what time does the restaurant begin serving dinner?

❸ How would you find out what the *soup du jour* is?

❹ What is served with each entrée except the Salad Nicoise?

❺ Would you expect to get a bigger portion of food if you order *hors d'oeuvres* or an *entrée*? Explain why.

❻ Do the *a la carte* items come with the main course?

❼ If you could order one item from each section on the menu, what would it be? What is something new you'd be willing to try? What is something you would never want to try?

❽ How does tipping work in this restaurant?

Have students complete the *Vocabulary Quick Check*.

Step 4
Discuss the *Did You Know?* information about borrowed words, the *Think About It!* question about gratuities, and the *Be Smart!* tip for dining out at restaurants.

Step 5
Now It's Your Turn
Have students work individually or with a partner to complete the *Now It's Your Turn* page.

Did You Know?
The English language uses many borrowed words from other languages such as French, Japanese, German, Spanish, and Italian. Here are some popular names of foods that English has adopted: hamburger, taco, sushi, and lasagna. What are some others you know?

Name _____ Date _____

Read a Restaurant Menu

Dinner Menu
❦ (served from 4PM) ❦

Hors d'Oeuvres
Escargot (snails) in garlic butter
Quiche with vegetables and cheese
Shrimp Cocktail

Soups
French Onion Soup
Soup du Jour

Entrées
Fried Chicken with mashed potatoes
Rack of Lamb with rice
Grilled Salmon with potatoes
Steak with fries
Stuffed Portobello Mushrooms
All the above served with salad and house dressing
Salad Nicoise with fresh tuna

A la carte
French fries   wild rice
mashed potatoes   grilled vegetables

Desserts
Sorbet • Chocolate Mousse • Fondue • Seasonal Fruits

18% Gratuity Added to the Bill

Words to Know

a la carte—means: *on the side*; food that can be ordered as separate items

appetizer—*a starter* or a small dish of food served at the beginning of the meal

beverages—drinks

cuisine—a style of food such as Mexican, Italian, or Japanese

entrée—the main dish

gratuity—tip (an amount of money paid to the waiter for service)

hors d'oeuvre—another word for *appetizer*, or a small portion of food

house—made by the restaurant as in *house dressing*

parties—groups of people eating together

sides—a la carte items; food that can be ordered separately

soup du jour—soup of the day

substitutions—switches

Vocabulary Quick Check

True or False

1. *Soup du jour* is a flavor of a soup.
   ❏ True   ❏ False

2. The waiter gives the customer a *gratuity*.
   ❏ True   ❏ False

3. *Hors d'oeuvres*, *starters*, and *appetizers* are synonyms.
   ❏ True   ❏ False

 Think About It!

Customers usually decide on the waiter's tip. Some restaurants, however, have a different policy. They automatically add the tip for the waiter to the bill. Do you agree or disagree with this policy? Explain why.

Be Smart!

Don't be shy at a restaurant. If you want to know what something means, just ask your waiter or waitress. It's the waitperson's job to answer questions about all the food on the menu.

Building Real-Life Reading Skills • © 2009 by Cindy Harris • Scholastic Teaching Resources

Name _____ Date _____

Read a Restaurant Menu

Step 1
Read the menu below.

River Cafe

Menu
Starters

Quesadilla tortilla with beans and cheese $6

Soup du jour $4

Mozzarella Sticks $7

Barbecue Ribs $8

Health Salad $6

Greek Salad $8

Caesar Salad $5

Entrees
served with House Salad (no substitutions)

Three Bean Vegetarian Chili $8

Lasagna with three cheeses $10

Teriyaki Salmon $14

Rib Eye Steak $17

Personal Pizza $10

A la carte
$3.50 each

French Fries · Cole Slaw · Roasted Potatoes
Steamed Vegetables · Rice Pilaf

Beverages
$1.50

Spring Water · Soda · House Lemonade · Iced Tea

15% Gratuity will be added to bills for parties of 6 or more.

Step 2
Answer these questions.

1. Under which category are salads listed on this menu?

_____

2. What is served with every dinner at this restaurant?

_____

3. How much is a side order of French Fries?

_____

4. If you don't eat meat or fish, what three entrees could you order?

_____

5. What is the most expensive entrée?

_____

6. Can you order orange juice at this restaurant?

_____

7. If you want French Fries instead of salad with your main course, can you switch? Why or why not?

_____

_____

8. Suppose a family of four is at this restaurant. Will the tip be added to the bill? Why or why not?

_____

_____

Write About It!

If you went to this restaurant, what would you order? Try to use two words from the *Words to Know* box as you describe your meal.

Read a Sports Schedule

LITTLE LEAGUE BASEBALL SCHEDULE

Division 2
Team Name: TIGERS

Game	Day	Date	Time	Location	Opponent
1	Sat	28-Mar	12:30 PM	Home	Cardinals
2	Thurs	2-Apr	5:30 PM	Home	Wolves
3	Tues	7-Apr	5:00 PM	Away	Blue Jays
4	Sat	18-Apr	11:00 AM	Home	Cubs
5	Thurs	23-Apr	5:30 PM	Away	Dodgers
6	Tues	28-Apr	5:00 PM	Away	Orioles
7	Sat	2-May	12:30 PM	Home	Cardinals
8	Thurs	7-May	6:00 PM	Away	Padres
9	Wed	13-May	5:00 PM	Home	Phillies
10	Sat	23-May	3:30 PM	Away	Blue Jays

Real-Life Scenario

The Sosas are a very busy family. All the kids in the family participate in after-school activities. Fourth grader Anthony is on a little league baseball team. The coach gave Anthony the team's schedule at the beginning of the season. Anthony's mom told Anthony that it was his job to keep track of his game schedule. Now, Anthony just has to figure out how to read it.

What's at Stake
Not missing any games.

Teach

Step 1
Set the Stage
- Read aloud the *Real-Life Scenario* and *What's at Stake*.
- Ask students to share about their after-school activities, and who keeps track of the schedule.

Step 2
Overview
- Review the vocabulary in the *Words to Know* box.
- Direct students to the *Sports Schedule*. Point out the heading of each column. Model how to read the schedule. For example, say: *Suppose it's Saturday, April 18, and I want to figure out the game schedule. I look in the column under the date and find April 18. Then I look at the column next to it to find out the time, the location, and the opponent for this game. I see that the game is at 11:00 at home and that we'll be playing against the Cubs.*

Step 3
Guided Questions
These are suggested questions to ask your students. Read them aloud.

❶ Where is game #3 being played—home or away?

❷ How many games are there in all? How many *home* games are there? How many *away* games are there?
❸ When do the Tigers play the Wolves?
❹ What month do the games begin? What month do they end?
❺ What time does game #6 start?
❻ Are most games in the morning or the afternoon?
❼ Which two teams do the Tigers play twice?
❽ On which three days of the week are most of the games played?

Have students complete the *Vocabulary Quick Check*.

Step 4
Discuss the *Did You Know?* sports fact and the *Think About It!* question.

Step 5
Now It's Your Turn
Have students work individually or with a partner to complete the *Now It's Your Turn* page.

Did You Know?
In the United States, the most popular team sports are football, baseball, basketball, and ice hockey. But in other countries, soccer is the most popular sport.

Name _____ Date _____

Read a Sports Schedule

LITTLE LEAGUE BASEBALL SCHEDULE

Division 2
Team Name: **TIGERS**

Game	Day	Date	Time	Location	Opponent
1	Sat	28-Mar	12:30 PM	Home	Cardinals
2	Thurs	2-Apr	5:30 PM	Home	Wolves
3	Tues	7-Apr	5:00 PM	Away	Blue Jays
4	Sat	18-Apr	11:00 AM	Home	Cubs
5	Thurs	23-Apr	5:30 PM	Away	Dodgers
6	Tues	28-Apr	5:00 PM	Away	Orioles
7	Sat	2-May	12:30 PM	Home	Cardinals
8	Thurs	7-May	6:00 PM	Away	Padres
9	Wed	13-May	5:00 PM	Home	Phillies
10	Sat	23-May	3:30 PM	Away	Blue Jays

Words to Know

away—refers to a game that is played on the other team's territory

division—a set of teams grouped together to play against each other

home—refers to a game that is played on the team's own field

opponent—someone or a team that plays against another

season—a specific time in the year when a sport is played

versus—against; (abbreviation **vs.**)

Vocabulary Quick Check

True or False

_____ 1. A **home** game is played on the other team's field.

_____ 2. An **opponent** competes against your team.

_____ 3. A **division** is made up of **seasons**.

Think About It!

Anthony wants to mark the game schedule in some way so he can keep track of which games he already played and which games are coming up. What would you suggest to him?

Name _____ Date _____

Read a Sports Schedule

**Glenview
Elementary School**

Division 1

Season Game Schedule

Teams	Opponent	Date	Time	Location
Sharks	Scorpions	Mon. May 5	4:00 PM	Away
Wolves	Lions	Wed. May 7	5:30 PM	Home
Sharks	Tigers	Mon. May 12	4:30 PM	Home
Wolves	Bears	Wed. May 14	5:00 PM	Home
Sharks	Dragons	Mon. May 19	4:30 PM	Away
Wolves	Scorpions	Wed. May 21	4:00 PM	Home
Sharks	Bears	Mon. June 1	5:30 PM	Home
Wolves	Tigers	Wed. June 2	5:00 PM	Away
Sharks	Lions	Mon. June 8	5:00 PM	Home
Wolves	Dragons	Wed. June 10	4:30 PM	Away
WOLVES	*SHARKS*	*Mon. June 15*	*5:00 PM*	*HOME*

Step 1
Read the soccer game schedule below for students at Glenview Elementary. Notice that there are two home teams.

Step 2
Answer these questions.

1. What are the names of the two teams at Glenview Elementary School?

   _____

2. How many different opponents are there in all? _____

3. On which days of the week do the games take place?

   _____

4. During which months of the year do the teams play?

   _____

5. How many games will the Sharks play at home? _____

6. What is the earliest time and the latest time that games begin?

   _____

7. What day of the week do the Wolves play their games?

   _____

8. How many away games will the Wolves play?

   _____

9. Which teams will play against each other in the final game?

   _____

10. What will be the location of the final game?

    _____

Write About It!
Write an activity schedule for yourself. Write the activity or activities you participate in, the days of the week you go, the time, and the location.

Building Real-Life Reading Skills • © 2009 by Cindy Harris • Scholastic Teaching Resources

Read a Lobby Directory

SKILLS:
- Reading for information
- Understanding and using directories

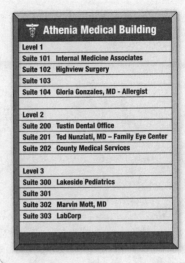

⚕ Athenia Medical Building

Level 1	
Suite 101	Internal Medicine Associates
Suite 102	Highview Surgery
Suite 103	
Suite 104	Gloria Gonzales, MD - Allergist
Level 2	
Suite 200	Tustin Dental Office
Suite 201	Ted Nunziati, MD – Family Eye Center
Suite 202	County Medical Services
Level 3	
Suite 300	Lakeside Pediatrics
Suite 301	
Suite 302	Marvin Mott, MD
Suite 303	LabCorp

Real-Life Scenario

Ethan and his mother race into the lobby of a medical building. They are late for Ethan's appointment at Dr. Nunziati, a new eye doctor. Just as they spot the lobby directory to figure out where to go, Ethan's mother realizes that she left her glasses in the car. She tells Ethan to look for the doctor's name in order to find out which floor the doctor is on, and what his office number is. But as Ethan scans the directory, he is immediately confused. It doesn't seem to be in any sort of order, and he can't figure out how to locate the information he needs.

What's at Stake

Getting to the office so that Ethan doesn't lose his appointment.

Teach

Step 1

Set the Stage
- Read aloud the *Real-Life Scenario* and *What's at Stake*.
- Ask students to brainstorm public places where they have seen directories. (*office buildings, museums, shopping malls*)

Step 2

Overview
- Review the vocabulary in the *Words to Know* box.
- Read through the *Lobby Directory* with students, line by line.
- Explain that directories can be organized in many different ways such as:
  - in alphabetical order
  - by floor
  - by office number
  - by category (such as "shoes" or "dentists")

Step 3

Guided Questions
These are suggested questions to ask your students. Read them aloud.

❶ In what order is this directory arranged?

❷ How many floors are there in this building?

❸ How many offices are in this particular building?

❹ Where is Dr. Nunziati's office and what is the name of his practice?

❺ What kind of doctor is Dr. Gonzales?

❻ Some suites don't have names next to them. Why do you think the names aren't there?

❼ Suppose you came to the building to see Dr. Kane, a dentist, and can't find his name on the directory. Would you still be able to figure out where to go? Why or why not?

Have students complete the *Vocabulary Quick Check*.

Step 4

Discuss the *Think About It!* question and the *Be Smart!* helpful hint.

Step 5

Now It's Your Turn
Have students work individually or with a partner to complete the *Now It's Your Turn* page.

Name _____ Date _____

Read a Lobby Directory

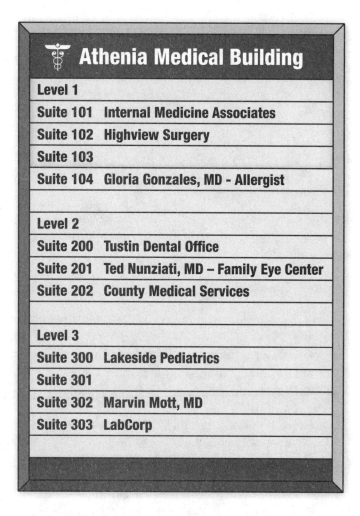

Athenia Medical Building

Level 1

Suite 101	Internal Medicine Associates
Suite 102	Highview Surgery
Suite 103	
Suite 104	Gloria Gonzales, MD - Allergist

Level 2

Suite 200	Tustin Dental Office
Suite 201	Ted Nunziati, MD – Family Eye Center
Suite 202	County Medical Services

Level 3

Suite 300	Lakeside Pediatrics
Suite 301	
Suite 302	Marvin Mott, MD
Suite 303	LabCorp

Words to Know

associates—partners

lobby—the main area near the entrance of a building that leads to other hallways or offices

directory—a listing of names and places in the building

MD—abbreviation for "medical doctor"

suite—set of offices or group of rooms

level—another word for "floor"

Vocabulary Quick Check

Complete each series with a word from the *Words to Know* box

1. catalog, list, _____

2. group, set, _____

3. hall, entrance, _____

 ## Think About It!

Let's say you were in charge of making a directory for an office building. What format would you use to organize the names and offices? Why would you choose this format?

Be Smart! _____

No matter how long a directory is, you can find what you're looking for, if you remember this... *first*, figure out how the directory is organized. For example, is it organized by floor or alphabetical order? Then, search for the name you need.

Building Real-Life Reading Skills • © 2009 by Cindy Harris • Scholastic Teaching Resources

Name _____ Date _____

Read a Lobby Directory

Step 1

Read the lobby directory for the city hall building.

Bloomfield City Hall Directory

First Level	Room
City Clerk	100
Fingerprinting	101
Mayor	108
Permits	105
Personnel Office	110
Police	102
Tax Collector	107

Second Level	Room
Health Clinic	204
Marriage Licenses	202
Passports	207
Recreation	209
Recycling	203
Senior Citizens Program	200

Step 2

Answer these questions.

1. In your own words, explain how this City Hall directory is arranged?

_____

2. How many floors are there in this building? _____

   How many rooms are there? _____

3. If you wanted to find out about joining the town's Little League baseball program, what room would you go to?

_____

4. What room would you go to for information about activities in town for your grandfather?

_____

5. If a person is told to go to Room 202, what does this person probably need to get?

_____

6. If you needed to report a crime, what floor and what room would you go to?

_____

7. Some children get their vaccinations at their city hall. What floor and what room would you go to for this?

_____

8. Do you think this directory is organized well? Why or why not?

_____

Write About It!

Make a directory for some of the classrooms and offices in your school. You may choose rooms such as the main office, the nurse's office, the art room, and the classrooms in your grade. Organize the directory in any manner you like.

Building Real-Life Reading Skills • © 2009 by Cindy Harris • Scholastic Teaching Resources

Read Instant-Food Directions

Real-Life Scenario

Taylor's favorite after-school snack is microwavable popcorn. Taylor asks his mother if he can make the popcorn by himself. Taylor's mother gives Taylor the popcorn bag and tells him to read the instructions on the bag. She tells Taylor that if he follows the directions correctly, and she sees that he knows exactly what to do, she'll allow him to make the popcorn on his own next time.

What's at Stake

Microwaving the popcorn correctly so that Taylor can make it on his own next time.

Teach

Step 1

Set the Stage
- Read aloud the *Real-Life Scenario* and *What's at Stake*.
- Ask students if they ever eat microwave popcorn at home. If so, who makes it?

Step 2

Overview
- Review the vocabulary in the *Words to Know* box.
- Direct students to the *Microwave Popping Instructions*. Explain that the instructions require you to follow a sequence of steps. The steps are usually numbered like these. Point out the numbered illustrations on the left that correspond with the step-by-step instructions.
- Read each step aloud.
- Make special note of the Helpful Hints and the Warning text.

Step 3

Guided Questions
These are suggested questions to ask your students. Read them aloud.

❶ What is the very first step you must do to make the popcorn?

❷ Describe how you should put the bag in the microwave.

❸ What is the suggested microwave time?

❹ How should you open up the bag when the popcorn is ready?

❺ What will happen if you microwave the bag for too long?

❻ Can you put the bag back in the microwave once it is done popping? Explain how you know this.

❼ How many helpful hints are there? Explain one of them in your own words.

Have students complete the *Vocabulary Quick Check*.

Step 4

Discuss the *Did You Know?* information and the *Be Smart!* warning.

Step 5

Now It's Your Turn
Have students work individually or with a partner to complete the *Now It's Your Turn* page.

Did You Know?

Microwave ovens vary in power. That's why the directions say to microwave the bag for 2 to 5 minutes. You should stay near the microwave while the popcorn is popping. If the popping slows down or stops, it means the popcorn is ready. Leaving the bag in the microwave too long will cause the popcorn to burn.

Name _____ Date _____

Read Instant-Food Directions

Step 1
Read the instant-food directions below.

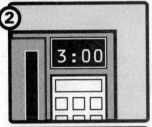

Microwave Popping Instructions

1. Remove plastic overwrap. Place the bag in the microwave. Make sure the side with these INSTRUCTIONS IS FACING UP.

2. Microwave on HIGH for 2 to 5 minutes. NEVER LEAVE MICROWAVE UNATTENDED. Listen carefully. Stop the microwave when popping slows to 2 to 3 seconds between pops. Don't overcook or the popcorn will scorch.

3. Handle the hot bag carefully. Open bag by tugging diagonally on two opposite corners. Keep away from face and be careful of hot steam.

Helpful Hints

1. For optimum flavor, shake the bag before opening to coat with salt and flavoring.

2. Don't stop and restart microwave.

WARNING: Do not reheat unpopped kernels

THIS SIDE UP

Large type and capital letters signal that this must be something very important.

Words to Know

kernel—the unpopped corn

optimum—best

overwrap—outer wrapping

scorch—burn

steam—hot water vapor

unattended—no one being present to watch

instant—food that can be made quickly

Vocabulary Quick Check
Synonyms and Antonyms

1. A synonym for *immediate* is _____.

2. The opposite of *worst* is _____.

3. A synonym for *hot vapor* is _____.

Be Smart!

When you take the cover off hot food, steam will escape. Steam can cause a severe burn. Keep your hands away from the opening you make in the package while the steam escapes.

Name _____ Date _____

Read Instant-Food Directions

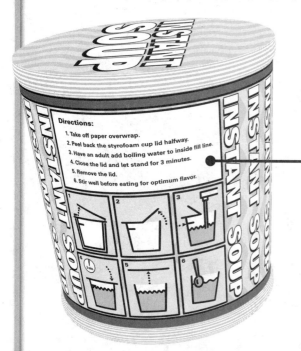

Step 1
Read the instant-food directions below.

Directions:
1. Take off paper overwrap.
2. Peel back the styrofoam cup lid halfway.
3. Have an adult add boiling water to inside fill line.
4. Close the lid.
5. Let stand for 3 minutes.
6. Remove lid.
7. Stir well before eating for optimum flavor.

Step 2
Answer these questions.

1. What is the first step you must do to prepare this soup?

   _____

2. How far back should you peel the lid?

   _____

3. How much water should you add to the cup?

   _____

4. What is the next step you must do after adding the water?

   _____

5. How long do you need to wait before you can eat the soup?

   _____

6. Why do you think it's necessary to stir the soup before eating it?

   _____

7. What do you think would happen if you only waited one minute before eating the soup?

   _____

8. What do you think would happen if you waited one hour before eating the soup?

   _____

Write About It!
Suppose you want to teach your friend how to make microwave popcorn. What are three important tips you would make sure you gave him or her.

Read **Parking Signs**

Real-Life Scenario

It's Sunday afternoon. Ryan and his grandfather are going to a special exhibit on Egyptian mummies at the museum in the city. By the time they arrive, the museum's parking lot is full. Grandpa says they'll have to park their car on the street. Ryan remembers from other trips to the city that there are lots of rules about where and when you can park a car. He also remembers that his father's car got towed once because he didn't read the signs carefully. Ryan's grandfather asks Ryan to help him as they search for a spot. The signs can be tricky, so they need to be read carefully.

What's at Stake

Getting a parking ticket or, worse, returning to find that the car has been towed away.

Teach

Step 1

Set the Stage

- Read aloud the *Real-Life Scenario* and *What's at Stake*.
- Ask students if they want to share any personal stories or experiences they've had with parking signs, meters, tickets, cars being towed away, etc.

Step 2

Overview

- Review the vocabulary in the *Words to Know* box.
- Read through each of the *Parking Signs* with students.
- Point out that every detail is critical and that parking signs must be read very carefully.

Step 3

Guided Questions

These are suggested questions to ask your students. Read them aloud.

❶ Look at Sign 1. When is it okay to park here?

❷ Why would a car get a ticket if it were parked next to Sign 2?

❸ Look at Sign 3 Can Ryan's grandfather park the car here?

❹ Look at Sign 4. Can Ryan's grandfather park the car here?

❺ Next to which sign can Ryan's grandfather never park the car?

❻ What do the arrows on the signs mean?

Have students complete the *Vocabulary Quick Check.*

Step 4

Discuss the *Did You Know?* trivia fact, the *Think About It!* question, and the *Be Smart!* suggestion.

Step 5

Now It's Your Turn

Have students work individually or with a partner to complete the *Now It's Your Turn* page.

Did You Know?

In the state of Wyoming, all street signs are printed in both English and the American sign language.

Name _____ Date _____

Read Parking Signs

① NO PARKING
7am – 6pm
Tues and Thurs

② BUS STOP
NO STANDING OR PARKING
ANYTIME

③ UNLOADING ZONE
NO PARKING
Mon – Sat
8am – 6pm

④ PERMIT PARKING ONLY
Monday – Friday

Words to Know

standing—stopped, as if you're parking, and waiting in the car

unloading—removing items from a truck or other vehicle

permit—special document or certificate giving permission

zone—an area

meter—a machine next to a parking space. A meter allows the driver of a car to park for a certain length of time after putting in money.

Vocabulary Quick Check

1. Another word for a zone is   ____ a. section   ____ b. price

2. Another word for a permit is   ____ a. trophy   ____ b. certificate

3. A parking meter measures   ____ a. time   ____ b. distance

Be Smart!

If you're ever in doubt about what a parking sign says, don't park there. It's better to find another spot than to risk getting a ticket or being towed away.

 ## Think About It!

If a sign says NO STANDING, can you park a car there? Why or why not?

Name _____   Date _____

Read Parking Signs

Step 1 Read the parking signs below.

Step 2

Answer these questions.

1. When can you park by sign #1?

   _____

   _____

2. What do you need to park by sign #1 at 2 PM?

   _____

3. Which sign never allows you to stop there or park there?

   _____

4. Which signs allow you to park there anytime you want on a Sunday?

   _____

   _____

5. Look at sign #2. What hours of the day can you park there?

   _____

6. Look at sign #4. If you park your car there at 9 AM on a Tuesday, what must you do in order not to get a ticket?

   _____

7. List two different days and times that it is free to park next to sign #4.

   _____

8. Which sign limits parking depending on the weather?

   _____

9. What do you think is the reason behind such a sign?

   _____

 Write About It!

In your own words, explain to someone what "No Standing" means on a sign.

Read an Amusement Park Operation & Rates Schedule

Real-Life Scenario

The Schmidts are getting ready for their family vacation trip. The Schmidts want their kids to understand that they have limited time to see everything—and a limited budget, too. So things will run smoothly, they are planning in advance where they will go and how long they will spend at each site. The kids made it clear that their number one priority is having time at *Funtime Amusement Park*. Using the park's online operational schedule and ticket rates, the Schmidts need to figure out when they'll go to the amusement park, and how much it will cost.

What's at Stake

Maximizing their fun so they'll have an awesome family vacation!

Teach

Step 1

Set the Stage

- Read aloud the *Real-Life Scenario* and *What's at Stake*.

- Ask students if they have ever seen a rate and operational schedule like this one, for an amusement park. Then take a poll. Ask students: *Who would want to try to figure out this schedule on your own? Who would prefer an adult to explain it to them?*

Step 2

Overview

- Review the vocabulary in the *Words to Know* box.

- Read the *Operation & Rates Schedule* with students.

- Direct students to the key below the three monthly calendars. Explain what the different colors/shading represent.

Step 3

Guided Questions

These are suggested questions to ask your students. Read them aloud.

❶ What is the regular admission price to the park?

❷ How much will a ticket cost for Kim Schmidt who is 5 years old?

❸ How old does Grandpa Schmidt need to be to get the senior citizen price?

❹ During which months and on which dates is the park always open until 9:00?

❺ Until what time is the park open during the last week of August?

❻ Why do you think the park is closed weekdays in September?

❼ The Schmidts' vacation budget allows them to buy one day's worth of tickets to the park. The kids really want to spend more time there. What does the park offer that would help them?

❽ Look at the Preview Plan. How does this offer work?

Have students complete the *Vocabulary Quick Check*.

Step 4

Discuss the *Think About It!* season-pass question and the *Be Smart!* helpful hint.

Step 5

Now It's Your Turn

Have students work individually or with a partner to complete the *Now It's Your Turn* page.

Name _____ Date _____

Read an Amusement Park Operation & Rates Schedule

Bob's FUNLAND

Rates

Regular Admission........................ $25.00
(ages 7 – 59)

Child Admission $17.00
(ages 3 – 6)

Senior Citizen Admission $15.00
(60 & older)

Ages 2 and under .... FREE

Season Tickets $75.00

Special Preview Plan:
A Night of Free Fun!

Do you want an extra night at the park for free? Here is how. Come to the park 3 hours prior to closing on any night. Buy a regular admission ticket to visit the park the next day. We'll let you in for a 3 hour preview of the park that night, and then we'll see you in the morning for a full day of fun!

Bob's FUNLAND

Closed — **Open 10 am – 9 pm** — **Open 10 am – 7 pm**

Words to Know

consecutive—following one after another with no break in between

rates—prices

admission—the fee you need to pay to enter

preview—to view or participate in advance

prior—before

senior citizen—a person 60 years of age or older

season ticket—a ticket that allows a person to enter the park as many times as desired without paying each time

Vocabulary Quick Check
Check the right box.

1. Are the third, fourth, and sixth of July **consecutive** days? ❏ yes ❏ no

2. Is breakfast **prior** to lunch? ❏ yes ❏ no

3. Do you pay an **admission** when you leave the park? ❏ yes ❏ no

Be Smart!

Always check the weather forecast before buying tickets to an amusement park. Many parks will not refund your money if the weather turns sour.

 ## Think About It!

For whom would it make the most sense to buy season tickets to the park? Explain what you think.

Name _____ Date _____

Read an Amusement Park Operation & Rates Schedule

Step 1 Read the rates and schedules for the Water Park.

Step 2
Answer these questions.

1. On what days is the water park closed?

   _____

2. What time is the park open until on weekends?

   _____

3. What time does the park open on weekdays?

   _____

4. What hours is the park open on July 4th?

   _____

5. How much would it cost for an adult to go to the park on a Thursday?

   _____

6. Is it cheaper to go to the park on a weekday or weekend? _____

7. How much is a child's admission to the park on Independence Day, July 4th?

   _____

8. Is there a senior citizen discount for this water park? _____

9. How much would it cost for a 5-year-old to go to the park on a Tuesday?

   _____

10. Let's say you plan to go to the water park three times this summer. If you're 9 years old, does it pay to buy a season pass or three regular admission tickets? Explain your answer.

    _____

    _____

Write About It!
Your family is going to the water park on a Sunday. Figure out how much it will cost for everyone in your family to go. Then figure out how much it would cost if you all went on a weekday instead. How much would you save?

Building Real-Life Reading Skills • © 2009 by Cindy Harris • Scholastic Teaching Resources

Read a Magazine Subscription Form

SKILLS:
- Completing a subscription form
- Analyzing information

Fill out and mail this reply card today!

YES! Send me a FREE Puzzle and Maze Minibook and 12 issues of *Kid Fun*.

Special Offer for New Subscribers Only!

Special if you order NOW:

○ 1 year (12 issues) $19   ○ 2 years (24 issues) $36   (REGULAR ANNUAL PRICE $25)

Child's Name _____

Buyer's Name _____

Address _____

City _____ State _____ Zip _____ Phone _____

○ payment enclosed   ○ bill me later   SATISFACTION GUARANTEED OR YOUR MONEY BACK!

Real-Life Scenario

Jeremy's friend has a subscription to an awesome magazine called *Kid Fun*. Jeremy decided to ask his mother if she would get him his own subscription. Jeremy's mom thought it was a wonderful idea. She thought he was just the right age for his first magazine subscription. Before she ordered it for him, however, she wanted Jeremy to find out the magazine's price and to fill out his own subscription form.

What's at Stake

Getting a subscription to a cool magazine.

Teach

Step 1

Set the Stage

Read aloud the *Real-Life Scenario* and *What's at Stake*.

- Ask students if they have their own subscriptions to a magazine. If so, which one?
- Ask students if they ever noticed the magazine subscription form in a magazine. Where was it?

Step 2

Overview

- Review the vocabulary in the *Words to Know* box.
- Read through the *Magazine Subscription Form* with students.
- Point out all the fine print and the areas of the card that need to be filled in.

Step 3

Guided Questions

These are suggested questions to ask your students. Read them aloud.

❶ What is the special price for a one-year subscription to *Kid Fun* if the subscriber orders the magazine now?

❷ What is the regular price for a one-year subscription?

❸ How much will a subscriber save on the one-year subscription by ordering it via the subscription form?

❹ How much is a two-year subscription?

❺ How many issues of the magazine will Jeremy receive if he orders a one-year subscription?

❻ Can you get the free minibook of puzzles if you already get the magazine? Why?

❼ Who has to pay the postage if you send back the subscription card?

Have students complete the *Vocabulary Quick Check*.

Step 4

Discuss the *Think About It!* question and the *Be Smart!* tip about advertising that uses the word "Free."

Step 5

Now It's Your Turn

Have students work individually or with a partner to complete the *Now It's Your Turn* page.

Name _____ Date _____

Read a Magazine Subscription Form

BUSINESS REPLY MAIL
FIRST CLASS MAIL   PERMIT NO. 5555

POSTAGE WILL BE PAID BY ADDRESSEE

NO POSTAGE
NECESSARY
IF MAILED
IN THE
UNITED STATES

Kid Fun
P.O. Box 402
My Town, CA 00000

Fill out and mail this reply card today!

YES! Send me a FREE Puzzle and Maze Minibook and 12 issues of **Kid Fun**.

Special Offer for New Subscribers Only!

Special if you order NOW:

○ 1 year (12 issues) $19   ○ 2 years (24 issues) $36   (Regular annual price $25)

Child's Name _____
Buyer's Name _____
Address_____
City _____ State _____ Zip _____ Phone _____

○ payment enclosed   ○ bill me later   Satisfaction guaranteed or your money back!

Words to Know

addressee—the person or company to whom the mail will be delivered

guarantee—a promise

subscription—money paid to receive a magazine over a period of time

subscriber—a person who orders a magazine

introductory—new and beginning

issue—a single copy of the magazine

annual—yearly

postage—the cost of sending a letter or package

Vocabulary Quick Check

True or False

1. **annual** means monthly
   ❏ True   ❏ False

2. the **addressee** is the person sending the postcard
   ❏ True   ❏ False

3. an **issue** is a single copy
   ❏ True   ❏ False

Be Smart! _____

Don't be fooled when you see the word "Free." Companies don't usually give away things for free. If they did, they wouldn't make money. So, if you see the word "Free" read further. Most often, you must buy something else to get the free item.

 Think About It!

What is the advantage of ordering a two-year subscription to the magazine?

_____
_____
_____
_____

Building Real-Life Reading Skills • © 2009 by Cindy Harris • Scholastic Teaching Resources

Name _____ Date _____

Read a Magazine Subscription Form

Step 1 Read the magazine subscription form below.

Get a cool compass FREE with your two-year subscription, PLUS two more surprise gifts during the year!

NO POSTAGE
NECESSARY
IF MAILED
IN THE
UNITED STATES

BUSINESS REPLY MAIL
FIRST CLASS MAIL   PERMIT NO. 5555
POSTAGE WILL BE PAID BY ADDRESSEE

Science for Kids
300 POST ROAD
SCIENCEVILLE, NY 12345

☑ **Yes!** I want to subscribe to **Science for Kids**

Name of Child receiving subscription _____ _____
First Name   Last Name

Street Address _____

City _____ State _____ Zip Code _____

Parent's Signature _____

Subscribe me for: ❑ 1 year ($12.50) ❑ 2 years ($21.00)
Annual subscription includes 11 issues. No publication in August.

❑ Send no money today. **Science for Kids** will bill me later.
Satisfaction guaranteed. If you are not completely satisfied, you may cancel at any time for a refund.

Science for Kids • *The magazine kids love to read!*

Step 2

Answer these questions.

1. How much is a one-year subscription?

_____

2. How much is a two-year subscription?

_____

3. Why is a two-year subscription a better deal?

_____

4. How many issues are in an annual subscription?

_____

5. In which month will you not receive the magazine?

_____

6. Are the surprise gifts really free? Why or why not?

_____

7. What must you do to receive the compass and surprise gifts?

_____

8. How much postage will Jeremy have to pay to mail the subscription card? Explain your answer.

_____

9. What does the magazine guarantee its readers?

_____

10. Do you have to pay before you get the first issue of the magazine?

_____

Write About It!

Imagine that you are ordering this magazine. Practice filling in the subscription form with your own information.

Read a Skin-Care Product Label

SKILL:
○ Reading and following procedural directions

Real-Life Scenario

The last time Meg went to the beach, she looked like a lobster the next day. Ouch! Now, Meg has plans to go to the beach for the day with her friend's family. Meg's mother gave her a bottle of sunscreen and reminded her to use it. Meg knows she'll be swimming most of the day, but she'll probably also play in the sand and throw a Frisbee around for a while, too. What does Meg have to do to make sure she doesn't get another nasty sunburn?

What's at Stake
Having a painful sunburn and damaged skin.

Teach

Step 1

Set the Stage
- Read aloud the *Real-Life Scenario* and *What's at Stake*.
- Ask students if they use sunscreen and if they know why it's so important to use it.

Step 2

Overview
- Review the vocabulary in the *Words to Know* box.
- Read through the entire label on the *SunBlock Lotion* bottle.
- Point out the headings for the **Directions** and the **Warnings**. Explain to students that the information here is bulleted so it's easy to read.
- Point out the Active Ingredients listed at the bottom of the label.

Step 3

Guided Questions
These are suggested questions to ask your students. Read them aloud.

❶ Does Meg need to reapply sunscreen after swimming?

❷ If she plays Frisbee for 20 minutes, does she need to reapply sunscreen?

❸ If she is in the water for two hours, does she need to reapply sunscreen?

❹ What should she do if the sunscreen gets in her eyes?

❺ If Meg gets a rash from the sunscreen, what does she need to do?

❻ The label says to *apply liberally*. What does this mean?

❼ Which reduces the sunscreen's effectiveness faster, water or perspiration?

Have students complete the *Vocabulary Quick Check*.

Step 4

Discuss the *Did You Know?* fact about skin cancer, the *Think About It!* question, and the *Be Smart!* tip.

Step 5

Now It's Your Turn
Have students work individually or with a partner to complete the *Now It's Your Turn* page.

Did You Know?

No matter how fair or dark you are, you should use sunscreen if you're out in the sun. More than 1 million people get skin cancer in the United States each year.

Name _____ Date _____

Read a Skin-Care Product Label

SunBlock Lotion SPF 30 provides excellent protection from the sun's harmful rays. Regular use of sunscreen helps prevent burning, premature aging, and the risk of skin damage. SunBlock Lotion SPF 30 has waterproof protection you can trust.

Directions
- Apply liberally to all exposed areas of the body.
- For maximum protection, apply 15 minutes before exposure to the sun.
- Reapply after 60 minutes of swimming.
- Reapply after 30 minutes of excessive perspiration.

Warnings
- For external use only!
- Discontinue use if irritation or a rash occurs.
- Avoid contact with eyes. If contact occurs, flush eyes thoroughly with water.
- Keep out of reach of small children.

Active Ingredients: Homosalate 15%, Octinoxate 7.5%, Titanium Dioxide 3%

Be Smart!
You can even get a sunburn on a cloudy day. That's because the clouds don't block the sun's UV (ultra violet) rays, which cause sunburns. Always use sunscreen!

Words to Know

apply—to put on

excessive—too much or extreme

exposed—uncovered

external—outside

irritation—pain or discomfort

flush—rinse

liberally—generously

maximum—the most

perspiration—sweat

repellent—something that keeps something else away

SPF—sun protection factor

waterproof—unaffected by water

Vocabulary Quick Check
Antonyms

Write a word from the Words to Know box that is the opposite of each word.

1. internal _____

2. covered up _____

3. minimum _____

 ## Think About It!

Think about your skin type and whether your skin tans or burns easily. Do you think you need a low, medium, or high SPF sunscreen? Explain why.

Building Real-Life Reading Skills • © 2009 by Cindy Harris • Scholastic Teaching Resources

Name _____ Date _____

Read a Skin-Care Product Label

Step 1

Read the Insect Repellent Label for Bugs Away! below.

Bugs Away! is an all-natural herbal insect repellent. No dangerous chemicals! It keeps away mosquitoes, ticks, gnats, and chiggers for up to 2 hours.

Directions:

Applying to Body: Hold spray bottle about 8 inches from skin or clothing and spray with a sweeping motion. Use enough spray to cover the exposed skin or clothing. Do not over-apply.

Applying to Face: Spray the palm of your hand with the spray. Then rub gently on your face, avoiding eye areas. Spread evenly for maximum protection. Do not apply to the mouth, lips, or eyes.

Warnings:

For external use only! Causes eye irritation. If spray gets in eyes, flush eyes thoroughly with water. Do not let very young children use without supervision. Test on small area of skin before use the first time in case of skin reaction.

Step 2

Answer these questions.

1. How long does *Bugs Away!* repellent keep insects away?

   _____

2. What are two types of bugs that *Bugs Away!* keeps away?

   _____

3. At what distance you should you hold the bottle before spraying?

   _____

4. In your own words, explain how you should apply *Bugs Away!* to your face.

   _____

5. Which word in the Warning section of the label means *discomfort*?

   _____

6. Why do you think the label says that young children shouldn't use the product without supervision?

   _____

Write About It!

What is another skin-care product that kids might apply to their skin by themselves? Name one good reason why it would be a good idea to read the label.

_____

Did You Know?

Mosquitoes are attracted to the carbon dioxide from your breath and skin. Insect repellent masks the carbon dioxide scent so the mosquitoes can't find you.

Building Real-Life Reading Skills • © 2009 by Cindy Harris • Scholastic Teaching Resources

Read a Nutrition Facts Label

Nutrition Facts
Serving Size 28g (About 10 chips)
Servings Per Container 20

Amount Per Serving	
Calories 200	Calories from Fat 90

% Daily Value*

Total Fat 11g	
Saturated Fat 2g	
Trans Fat 0g	
Cholesterol 1g	
Sodium 90mg	
Total Carbohydrate 19g	
Dietary Fiber 2g	
Sugars 1g	
Protein 3g	

Vitamin A 0%	Vitamin C 0%
Calcium 4%	Iron 2%

Real-Life Scenario

Jake just went for his yearly checkup. Dr. Kramer told Jake that he has to exercise more and develop better eating habits. She suggested that Jake cut down on foods that are high in fat, sugar, and cholesterol. Dr. Kramer explained to Jake that he can begin to manage his own diet if he learns how to read the Nutrition Facts labels that are on food packages. Some foods, she explained, are better choices than others.

What's at Stake
Jake's health.

Teach

Step 1
Set the Stage
- Read aloud the *Real-Life Scenario* and *What's at Stake*.
- Discuss with students how some foods masquerade as healthy snack choices—like granola bars that are really candy bars, and fruit roll ups that are really candy, not fruit. Invite students to talk about snacks they eat and whether or not they think these snacks have good nutritional value.

Step 2
Overview
- Review the vocabulary in the *Words to Know* box.
- Direct students to the Nutrition Facts Label. If possible, show students real samples of nutrition facts labels from food packages.
- Explain that a nutrition facts label tells what nutrients are in a food item and how much of those nutrients are found in one serving.
- Tell students that a **serving size** is often not the whole package. The facts label tells you how many servings are in the package. Unless the package is very small, like a snack size portion, the package will contain more than one serving.
- Nutrition labels can help people compare two or more foods and make choices about what they want to eat.
- Explain that daily value numbers on nutrition facts labels are based on a 2,000 calorie daily diet.

Step 3
Guided Questions
These are suggested questions to ask your students. Read them aloud.

❶ Which snack has more calories per serving?
❷ Which snack has more cholesterol per serving?
❸ How many cheese tortilla chips make one serving? How many pretzels make one serving?
❹ Which snack has less fat?
❺ Which snack has more fiber?

Have students complete the *Vocabulary Quick Check*.

Step 4
Discuss the *Did You Know?* law about nutrition facts labels, the *Think About It!* question, and the *Be Smart!* guide about nutrient percentages.

Step 5
Now It's Your Turn
Have students work individually or with a partner to complete the *Now It's Your Turn* page.

Did You Know?
By law, food products must have nutrition facts labels. The labels must list these nutrients: *fat, saturated fat, cholesterol, total carbohydrate, fiber, sugars, protein, Vitamin A, Vitamin C, calcium,* and *iron content.*

Name _____ Date _____

Read a Nutrition Facts Label

Nacho Cheese Tortilla Chips

Nutrition Facts	
Serving Size 28g (About 10 chips)	
Servings Per Container 20	
Amount Per Serving	
Calories 200	Calories from Fat 90
	% Daily Value*
Total Fat 11g	
Saturated Fat 2g	
Trans Fat 0g	
Cholesterol 1g	
Sodium 90mg	
Total Carbohydrate 19g	
Dietary Fiber 2g	
Sugars 1g	
Protein 3g	
Vitamin A 0% • Vitamin C 0%	
Calcium 4% • Iron 2%	

Pretzels

Nutrition Facts	
Serving Size 28g (About 32 pretzels)	
Servings Per Container About 15	
Amount Per Serving	
Calories 100	Calories from Fat 0
	% Daily Value*
Total Fat 0g	
Saturated Fat 0g	
Trans Fat 0g	
Cholesterol 0g	
Sodium 350mg	
Total Carbohydrate 24g	
Dietary Fiber Less than 1g	
Sugars 1g	
Protein 3g	
Vitamin A 0% • Vitamin C 0%	
Calcium 4% • Iron 8%	

Vocabulary Quick Check

Choose the correct word to complete each sentence.

sodium • calories • cholesterol

1. The amount of energy in a food is the food's

   _____.

2. Only foods made from animal products contain

   _____.

3. The amount of salt in a food is the

   _____ content.

Be Smart!

Here is an easy guide to understanding percentages on nutrition facts labels:

5% or less of a nutrient is low!

20% or more of a nutrient is high!

Words to Know

Gram—unit of measurement of weight

Serving size—a measured amount of a food or drink

Servings per container—how many servings are in one package

% of Daily Value—the percentage or amount of recommended daily nutrients in one serving

Calorie—a unit of energy

Total fat—the entire amount of fat

Saturated Fat—an unhealthy fat for the heart

Trans fat—fat that is unhealthy for the heart

Cholesterol—a substance found only in animal products

Sodium—salt content

Total carbohydrate—gives your muscles and brain energy

Dietary fiber—helps with digestion

Protein—a fundamental substance that builds muscles and fights infection

 ## Think About It!

Dr. Kramer wants Jake to avoid foods that are high in fat, cholesterol, and sugar. Do you think Dr. Kramer would approve of Jake's choice to eat tortilla chips? Why or why not?

Building Real-Life Reading Skills • © 2009 by Cindy Harris • Scholastic Teaching Resources

Name _____ Date _____

Read a Nutrition Facts Label

Step 1
Read the Nutrition Facts
Labels to the right.

Whole Milk
Serving Size 8 fl oz (240mL)
Servings Per Container 2

Amount Per Serving	
Calories 150	Calories from Fat 70
	% Daily Value*
Total Fat 8g	**12%**
Saturated Fat 5g	**25%**
Cholesterol 35mg	**12%**
Sodium 125mg	**5%**
Total Carbohydrate 12g	**4%**
Dietary Fiber 0g	**0%**
Sugars 11g	
Protein 8g	

Vitamin A 6% •	Vitamin C 4%

Calcium 30% • Iron 0% • Vitamin D 25%

Skim Milk
Serving Size 8 fl oz (240mL)
Servings Per Container 2

Amount Per Serving	
Calories 80	Calories from Fat 0
	% Daily Value*
Total Fat 0g	**0%**
Saturated Fat 0g	**0%**
Cholesterol less than 5mg	**1%**
Sodium 130mg	**5%**
Total Carbohydrate 12g	**4%**
Dietary Fiber 0g	**0%**
Sugars 11g	
Protein 8g	

Vitamin A 8% •	Vitamin C 4%

Calcium 30% • Iron 0% • Vitamin D 25%

Step 2 Answer these questions.
Whole Milk versus Skim Milk

1. What is a serving size of milk? _____

2. How many servings come in a container?
   _____

3. Does whole milk or skim milk have more calories?
   _____

4. What is the total fat of whole milk? _____

   What is the total fat of skim milk? _____

5. How much saturated fat is in a serving of whole milk?

   _____

   How much saturated fat is in a serving of skim milk?

   _____

6. Which type of milk has more cholesterol?

   _____

7. Which nutrition facts are not the same for whole milk and skim milk? _____
   a. fiber and sugar content
   b. protein and total carbohydrate content
   c. Vitamin C and Vitamin A content

8. How many grams of protein are found in a cup of milk?

   _____

9. What percentage of your daily calcium needs will a cup of milk give you?

   _____

10. Which type of milk has more Vitamin A?

   _____

Write About It!
In your own words, tell what you think is the major difference between whole milk and skim milk.
Which type of milk do you prefer to drink and why?

Read Merchandise Tags

58063 6724444
M (8)
RED
2601
Suggested Retail Price:
$39.99
OUR PRICE:
$29.99

Real-Life Scenario

Cho is hoping to buy her mother a sweater for Mother's Day. While in the department store, Cho picked out a few pretty sweaters. But when she showed them to Mia, her older sister, Mia shook her head and said none of them would fit. Cho forgot that she had to pick out the right size. She asked Mia to help her learn how to read the merchandise tags.

What's at Stake
Buying the wrong size and having to return the clothing.

Teach

Step 1
Set the Stage
• Read aloud the *Real-Life Scenario* and *What's at Stake*.
• Tell students to imagine they're shopping for a shirt. Can they think of two places on the garment that they can look to find out its size? (*the garment tag* and *the inside collar tag*)

Step 2
Overview
• Review the vocabulary in the *Words and Abbreviations to Know* box.
• Read the *Merchandise Tags* with students.
• Explain to students that merchandise tags usually hang from a garment and are often attached by a plastic string. Sometimes the tag is connected to the inner tag or label of the garment.

Step 3
Guided Questions
These are suggested questions to ask your students. Read them aloud.

❶ Look at Tag #1. What size is this item?
❷ Look at Tag #1. What is the price of this item?
❸ Look at Tag #1. Where was this item made?
❹ Look at Tag #2. What color is this item?
❺ Look at Tag #2. What is the size and price of this item?

❻ Look at Tag #2. What is style number of this item?
❼ Look at Tag #2. What is the brand name on this item?

Have students complete the *Vocabulary Quick Check*.

Step 4
Discuss the *Did You Know?* fact, the *Think About It!* question, and the *Be Smart!* tip.

Step 5
Now It's Your Turn
Have students work individually or with a partner to complete the *Now It's Your Turn* page.

Did You Know?
Many stores use standard sizes to size their clothing. If you learn your size, you'll have an easy time picking out clothing in your size. Here is a general size chart to help you.

age 4–6	**XS** = extra small = size 4/5
age 6–8	**S** = small = size 6/7
age 8–9	**M** = medium = size 8
age 10–12	**L** = large = size 10/12
age 12–14	**XL** = extra large = size 14/16

Name _____ Date _____

Read Merchandise Tags

BROWN TEE SHIRT
XL (14/16)

$6.99

90320   06704

Style 58943 • Made in China

Tag #1

KIDCITY
BRAND

Chino Pants 9875
Size: M
Color: Blue

00   1003   584

$14.99

Tag #2

Words and Abbreviations to Know

bar code—a machine-readable code in the pattern of numbers and a pattern of lines

husky—bigger clothing size; may be abbreviated with an H (size 10H)

merchandise—goods that are bought and sold

slim—slimmer clothing size; may be abbreviated with an S (size 10S)

XS—extra small

S—small

M—medium

L—large

XL—extra large

XXL—extra, extra large

Think About It!

Some clothing items, such as hats and scarves, are labeled "One Size Fits All." What do you think "One Size Fits All" really means?

Vocabulary Quick Check
Match the Abbreviations

XS	medium
M	size 14 husky
XXL	extra small
12S	extra, extra large
14H	size 12 slim

Be Smart!

When you are in a store that carries both child and adult sizes, make sure you look in the right department and read the tags carefully. An adult small is not the same as a child's size small.

Name _____ Date _____

Read Merchandise Tags

Step 1 Read the merchandise tags.

Tag #1 —

COATSforYOU.com

STYLE:
CP4301

COLOR:
Sky Blue

SIZE:
10/12

PRICE
$25.00

58063 6724444

M (8)
RED

2601

Suggested Retail Price:
$39.99

OUR PRICE:
$29.99

Tag #2 —

Step 2 Answer these questions.

1. Look at Tag #1. What size is this item?

    _____

2. Look at Tag #1. What color is this item?

    _____

3. Look at Tag #1. What type of clothing is this item?

    _____

4. Look at Tag #1. What is the item's price?

    _____

5. Look at Tag #1. What is the brand name on this item?

    _____

6. Look at Tag #2. What size is this item?

    _____

7. Look at Tag #2. What color is this item?

    _____

8. Look at Tag #2. What is the store's price for this item?

    _____

9. Look at Tag #2. How much does the store save you?

    _____

10. Look at Tag #2. What is the style number?

    _____

Write About It!

Make your own merchandise tag for a shirt, pair of pants, etc. Use the sample tags in this lesson as examples. Then give the tag to another student in your class. Ask the student two questions about your tag such as: *What color is this shirt? What size is it?* See if your partner can read the tag and answer your questions.

Building Real-Life Reading Skills • © 2009 by Cindy Harris • Scholastic Teaching Resources

Read an Ingredients List

Nutrition Facts
Serving Size 8 fl oz (240mL)
Servings Per Container 2

Amount Per Serving

Calories 150   Calories from Fat 70

% Daily Value*

Total Fat 8g	**12%**
Saturated Fat 2g	**10%**
Cholesterol 0mg	**0%**
Sodium 230mg	**10%**
Total Carbohydrate 18g	**6%**
Dietary Fiber less than 1g	**0%**
Sugars 2g	
Protein 2g	

INGREDIENTS: STRAWBERRY FILLING (STRAWBERRIES, APPLES, CONCENTRATED PEAR JUICE), TAPIOCA STARCH, SUGAR, VEGETABLE GLYCERIN, WHEAT FLOUR, ROLLED OATS, VEGETABLE OIL (CANOLA OIL AND/OR SOYBEAN OIL), WHEAT GLUTEN, WHEAT BRAN, SOY LECITHIN, NATURAL FLAVORS, HONEY, SKIMMED MILK POWDER, WHOLE MILK POWDER, BAKING SODA, SODIUM BENZOATE [A PRESERVATIVE], SALT, ARTIFICIAL VANILLA FLAVORING.
MAY CONTAIN TRACES OF PEANUTS.
MADE ON EQUIPMENT THAT PROCESS FOOD MADE WITH PEANUTS OR PEANUT DERIVATIVES.

Real-Life Scenario

Tyron had a sleepover at his friend's house. In the morning, Tyron wants a cereal bar for breakfast. But Tyron has to be very careful when he eats anything prepackaged. That's because he, like many kids, is highly allergic to peanuts. Before he eats any packaged food, he must check the list of ingredients. Tyron is on the lookout for any mention of peanuts, peanut oil, and peanut derivatives. He must also check the label to see if the food he wants to eat was processed on equipment that manufactures food containing peanuts.

What's at Stake

Tyron's life! Tyron could have a severe allergic reaction if he eats peanuts or something that has traces of peanuts in it.

Teach

Step 1

Set the Stage

- Read aloud the *Real-Life Scenario* and *What's at Stake*.
- Ask students if they can think of another scenario, similar to Tyron's, in which someone would need to read an ingredients list.

Step 2

Overview

- Review the vocabulary in the *Words to Know* box.
- Read the *Ingredients List* with students, ingredient by ingredient.
- Explain that the ingredients list appears as a long running list, like a paragraph and is usually found under, or next to, the *Nutrition Facts* box.
- The word **ingredients** is usually in bold type or all capital letters so that it is easy to spot.
- An ingredients list names every ingredient found in the product.
- Ingredients are listed in the order of most abundant ingredient to the least abundant ingredient.
- Words in parentheses tell the exact ingredients found within a particular ingredient. For example: *Enriched wheat flour (wheat flour, niacin, iron, riboflavin,* and *folic acid)* contains the ingredients listed within the parentheses.

Step 3

Guided Questions

These are suggested questions to ask your students. Read them aloud.

❶ What is the second most abundant ingredient in this type of cereal bar?

❷ Do these cereal bars contain more oil or sugar? How do you know?

❸ How many ingredients are in this cereal bar?

❹ Look carefully at the ingredients list and its warnings. Is this a food that Tyron can eat? Explain why or why not.

❺ What does it mean that the cereal bars contain canola *and/or* soybean oil?

Have students complete the *Vocabulary Quick Check.*

Step 4

Discuss the *Did You Know?* fact, the *Think About It!* questions and the *Be Smart!* tip about sugars.

Step 5

Now It's Your Turn

Have students work individually or with a partner to complete the *Now It's Your Turn* page.

Did You Know?

When an ingredients list is very long, the first two or three ingredients are usually the main ingredients.

Name _____ Date _____

Read an Ingredients List

Nutrition Facts

Serving Size 8 fl oz (240mL)
Servings Per Container 2

Amount Per Serving

Calories 150 Calories from Fat 70

% Daily Value*

Total Fat 8g	**12%**
Saturated Fat 2g	**10%**
Cholesterol 0mg	**0%**
Sodium 230mg	**10%**
Total Carbohydrate 18g	**6%**
Dietary Fiber less than 1g	**0%**
Sugars 2g	
Protein 2g	

INGREDIENTS: STRAWBERRY FILLING (STRAWBERRIES, APPLES, CONCENTRATED PEAR JUICE), TAPIOCA STARCH, SUGAR, VEGETABLE GLYCERIN, WHEAT FLOUR, ROLLED OATS, VEGETABLE OIL (CANOLA OIL AND/OR SOYBEAN OIL), WHEAT GLUTEN, WHEAT BRAN, SOY LECITHIN, NATURAL FLAVORS, HONEY, SKIMMED MILK POWDER, WHOLE MILK POWDER, BAKING SODA, SODIUM BENZOATE [A PRESERVATIVE], SALT, ARTIFICIAL VANILLA FLAVORING.

**MAY CONTAIN TRACES OF PEANUTS.
MADE ON EQUIPMENT THAT PROCESS FOOD
MADE WITH PEANUTS OR PEANUT DERIVATIVES.**

Words to Know

derivative—something that is obtained from a main source
  Example: peanut oil is a derivative of peanuts

ingredient—a food or food substance that's used to make a particular food
  Example: flour is an ingredient in crackers

enriched—improved by adding good things such as vitamins

natural *flavors*—flavors found in nature

artificial *flavors*—flavors made by people

processes—makes or manufactures

preservative—something in a food, usually a chemical, that prevents a food from spoiling

Think About It!

- *Why is it important to read the items in parentheses in an ingredients list?*

- *What could you do to find out what the natural flavors are in this cereal bar?*

Vocabulary Quick Check
In an Ingredients List

1. **traces** means
   a. bits **b.** footprints **c.** lines

2. **artificial** means
   a. plastic **b.** man-made **c.** real

3. **enriched** means
   a. wealthy **b.** added **c.** delicious

Be Smart!

Sugar goes by many names on ingredients labels. Here are some of them: *corn syrup, honey, malto-dextrin, corn sweeteners*, and *molasses* as well as any ingredient ending in *–ose*, such as *fructose* and *dextrose*.

Building Real-Life Reading Skills • © 2009 by Cindy Harris • Scholastic Teaching Resources

Name _____ Date _____

Read an Ingredients List

Step 1

Find the ingredients list and *read* the ingredients list.

Nutrition Facts

Serving Size 8 fl oz (240mL)
Servings Per Container 2

Amount Per Serving

Calories 150	Calories from Fat 70	

	% Daily Value*
Total Fat 8g	**12%**
Saturated Fat 2g	**10%**
Cholesterol 0mg	**0%**
Sodium 230mg	**10%**
Total Carbohydrate 18g	**6%**
Dietary Fiber less than 1g	**0%**
Sugars 2g	
Protein 2g	

INGREDIENTS: ENRICHED **WHEAT** FLOUR (**WHEAT** FLOUR, NIACIN, REDUCED IRON, THIAMIN MONONITRATE, RIBOFLAVIN, AND FOLIC ACID), PARTIALLY HYDROGENATED **VEGETABLE** OIL SHORTENING (CONTAINS ONE OR MORE OF THE FOLLOWING: **SOYBEAN** OIL, COTTONSEED OIL), SUGAR, HIGH FRUCTOSE CORN SYRUP. CONTAINS TWO PERCENT OR LESS OF: SALT, AMMONIUM BICARBONATE, SODIUM BICARBONATE, MONCALCIUM PHOSPHATE, SOY LECITHIN (AN EMULSIFIER), AND SODIUM SULFITE. **CONTAINS: SOYBEAN, WHEAT.**

Step 2

Answer these questions.

1. What is the main ingredient in this cracker?

_____

2. What sub-ingredients are found in this ingredient?

_____

3. If a person is allergic to soy, is it safe to eat this product? Why or why not?

_____

4. Can a person who is allergic to peanuts eat this kind of cracker? How do you know?

_____

5. What is something that the wheat flour is enriched with?

_____

6. This cracker contains 2% Daily Value or less of certain ingredients. Name two of them.

_____

7. Why do you think certain ingredients are listed in bold type?

_____

Write About It!

What is something you learned about ingredients lists that you didn't know before?

_____

_____

51

Read a Toy-Store Flyer

Toy World

FREE Bike Helmet
$19⁹⁹ Value
with ANY bicycle purchase $99 or more.
* Limited quantities available. Sorry, no rain checks.
SELECTION MAY VARY BY STORE.

FREE
Handheld Game
$14⁹⁹ Value
when you buy 2 or more cartridges.
IN STORE ONLY.

A Toy World exclusive!
$19⁹⁹
after $5 rebate
Super Speed Racing Scooter
SALE PRICES VALID OCTOBER 5-11

Real-Life Scenario

Isabel's relatives gave her money for her birthday. After her party, Isabel counted up all the money from the gifts she received. She had a total of $65. When her favorite toy store's flyer came in the mail the next day, Isabel got really excited. She flipped through the pages, making note of all the things she wanted to buy. Lots of things were on sale, too! But all the "special deals" and fine print made the flyer kind of confusing. Isabel wasn't sure what toys she had enough money for or just how many things she'd be able to buy.

What's at Stake

Figuring out what she can buy with her birthday money.

Teach

Step 1
Set the Stage
- Read aloud the *Real-Life Scenario* and *What's at Stake*.
- Ask students if they ever looked through a toy-store flyer that came in the mail or newspaper.

Step 2
Overview
- Review the vocabulary in the *Words to Know* box.
- Point out that flyers and advertisements often have a great deal of *fine print*. Explain to students that the *fine print* is extremely important and should not be skipped over.
- Explain all the fine print within the context of the ad.

Step 3
Guided Questions
These are suggested questions to ask your students. Read them aloud.

❶ How can Isabel get a free bike helmet? How much is the helmet really worth?

❷ What does Isabel have to do to get a free Handheld Game?

❸ What do the words "in store only" mean?

❹ Can a customer get the Super Speed Racing Scooter at another toy store? How do you know?

❺ How much does the Super Speed Racing Scooter cost?

Have students complete the *Vocabulary Quick Check*.

Step 4
Discuss the *Did You Know?* fact about Lego, the *Think About It!* question, and the *Be Smart!* tip about FREE things.

Step 5
Now It's Your Turn
Have students work individually or with a partner to complete the *Now It's Your Turn* page.

Did You Know?
Lego is one of the most popular toys. The famous interlocking blocks were first manufactured in 1949, and since then over 20,000,000,000 have been made per year—that's more than 600 Lego pieces per second!

Name _____ Date _____

Read a Toy-Store Flyer

Toy World

FREE Bike Helmet

$19⁹⁹ Value

with ANY bicycle purchase $99 or more.

* Limited quantities available. Sorry, no rain checks.

SELECTION MAY VARY BY STORE.

FREE

Handheld Game

$14⁹⁹ Value

when you buy 2 or more cartridges.

IN STORE ONLY.

A Toy World exclusive!

$19⁹⁹

after $5 rebate

Super
Speed Racing Scooter

SALE PRICES VALID OCTOBER 5-11

Words to Know

exclusive—special for only that store

fine print—small print

limited quantities—only a certain amount

rain check—a ticket, or slip of paper, that guarantees you that if a sale item is sold out, you can buy it at a later date and pay the sale price.

rebate—a partial refund or discount

substitutions—switches or exchanges

valid—in effect

💡 Think About It!

Why would a store advertise that they have only limited quantities of an item?

Vocabulary Quick Check

1. Is **fine print** large print or small print on an advertisement?

_____

2. Is a **rebate** money you owe or money that's refunded to you?

_____

3. Is a **rain check** a guarantee or a check you receive in the mail?

_____

Be Smart!

Don't be fooled! Always read the fine print on a flyer! Big print words like FREE are meant to grab your attention. The fine print tells you the real deal.

Name _____ Date _____

Read a Toy-Store Flyer

Step 1
Read the Toy Store Flyer below.

Toy World

Save $10
on these MP3 Players

SALE $39⁹⁹

was $49⁹⁹

Stock up Now!
New DVD movies only
$9⁹⁹ after $10 mail in rebate.
Limited Quantities. Sorry no rain-checks.
Selection may vary by store.

Super Gerbil
Silly Socks
The Worst Sleepover
My Friend Beeper
Camping 101

Buy 1 Get 1 FREE
on these games*
Choose from **Tic Tac Toe, Bingo, Checkers, Chess, and Marbles**
$7⁹⁹ No substitutions.
SHOP IN STORE OR ONLINE.
SALE PRICES VALID JANUARY 5–13.

Step 2
Answer these questions.

1. What is the sale price for an MP3 player? _____

2. What was the original price for the MP3 player? _____

3. Which games are included in the *Buy 1, Get 1 Free* offer?

   _____

   _____

4. What does *No substitutions* mean for the *Buy 1, Get 1 Free* games?

   _____

   _____

5. Will all stores have the same DVD movie selection? _____

   How do you know?

   _____

6. How much will you have to pay upfront for the DVD movie?

   _____

7. After the rebate for the DVD movies, how much will you get back in the mail?

   _____

8. From what day to what day does is this sale going on?

   _____

Write About It!
Suppose you had $75 to spend on toys. Look at the advertisements on this page and on page 53, then do the following:
1. Make a list of the items you want to buy.
2. Add up the prices. How much will they all cost?
3. How much would you save by buying these items during the advertised sale time?
4. How much money will you have leftover from the $75, or how much more money will you need to buy everything on your list?

Building Real-Life Reading Skills • © 2009 by Cindy Harris • Scholastic Teaching Resources

Read Clothing-Care Labels

100% Cotton
Machine Wash
Bleach When Necessary
Tumble Dry

MACHINE WASH   IRON   DRY   BLEACH

Real-Life Scenario

Jenny's mother has a new job and now works full time. With less time for household work, she needs Jenny to help out more. One of Jenny's new chores is to sort the family's laundry. Her mom asked her to put the dirty clothes into three piles—one for colored clothes, one for white clothes, and one for dry-clean clothes. She told Jenny that this will speed up the time it takes to do the wash. She explained to Jenny that if clothes end up in the wrong pile, they could get ruined.

What's at Stake

Not ruining any clothes and getting the job done right.

Teach

Step 1

Set the Stage

• Read aloud the *Real-Life Scenario* and *What's at Stake*.

• Ask students if they know where to find the washing instructions for a garment.

Step 2

Overview

• Review the vocabulary in the *Words to Know* box.

• Direct students to the *Clothing-Care Labels* and icons. Explain that different garments are made of different fabrics. Inside each garment, on a tag, is a washing label. This label can be found at the neck or back seam of the garment, or inside the garment, lower down, by a seam. The washing label has instructions and/or icons that explain how the garment should be washed.

• You may also take the opportunity to discuss the difference between washing whites, colors, and dry-clean clothing. Whites get cleaner in hot water and white clothing can be bleached. Colored clothing gets washed in cold water. The dyes in colored clothing can run in hot water. Dry-clean clothing must be sent to the dry cleaner and cannot be put in the washing machine.

Step 3

Guided Questions

These are suggested questions to ask your students. Read them aloud.

❶ What water temperature should Jenny use to wash her shirt?

❷ When Jenny sorts the wash, what pile should she put her red shirt in: with the whites, colors, or dry-clean clothes?

❸ When do you think a warm iron might be necessary?

❹ Based on these labels, what is a fabric that often requires dry cleaning?

❺ What does an X mean on a fabric-care symbol?

Have students complete the *Vocabulary Quick Check*.

Step 4

Discuss the *Did You Know?* fact, the *Think About It!* question, and the *Be Smart!* tip.

Step 5

Now It's Your Turn

Have students work individually or with a partner to complete the *Now It's Your Turn* page.

Did You Know?

Dry cleaning is a cleaning process for clothes that uses chemicals called solvents to get out the dirt. Dry-clean clothing is not cleaned with water.

Name _____ Date _____

Read Clothing-Care Labels

MACHINE WASH	BLEACH	TUMBLE DRY	DRY	IRON	DRY CLEAN

Jenny's Red Shirt　　　**Mom's Sweater**

This is the fabric that was used

This means the garment needs to be put in the washing machine in cold water

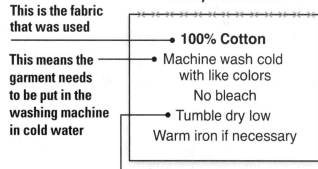

100% Cotton
Machine wash cold with like colors
No bleach
Tumble dry low
Warm iron if necessary

This means the garment should be put in the dryer on a low heat setting

**80% Wool
20% Cotton**
Dry Clean Only

This means the garment can not get wet— it doesn't go in the washer or the dryer

Words to Know

bleach—a chemical that removes color

detergent—a liquid or powder that is used to clean clothing

dry clean—a commercial process by which dirt is removed from clothing using chemicals.

fabric—a material that clothing is made from

garment—an item of clothing

hang dry—hang up to dry

machine wash—the process of using a washing machine, water, and detergent.

tumble dry—put in the drying machine

Vocabulary Quick Check
True or False

____ 1. Bleach gets your colored clothes clean.

____ 2. Dry-clean clothes get washed in cold water.

____ 3. Tumble dry means the garment can be dried in the dryer.

💡 Think About It!

Whites need to be washed in hot water. Color clothes need to be washed in cold water. What effect do you think the water temperature has?

Be Smart!

Never put a dry-clean garment into the washing machine or dryer. You can completely ruin it!

Building Real-Life Reading Skills • © 2009 by Cindy Harris • Scholastic Teaching Resources

Name _____ Date _____

Read Clothing-Care Labels

Step 1
Read the clothing labels and washing instructions.

100% Cotton
Machine Wash
Bleach When Necessary
Tumble Dry

MACHINE WASH   IRON   DRY   BLEACH

Label #1

45% Wool
55% Polyester

Machine Wash
Cold Water
Wash Separately
Gentle Cycle
Hang to Dry

Label #2

100% Silk
Dry Clean Only

Label #3

Step 2   Answer these questions.

1. Look at Label #1. What material is the garment made of?

   _____

2. Give an example of when it might be necessary to use bleach on this garment.

   _____

3. Look at Label #2. How should this garment be washed?

   _____

4. What does a symbol with an X through it mean?

   _____

5. How should you dry garment #2?

   _____

6. Look at Label #3. What fabric is this garment made of?

   _____

7. How should you clean this garment?

   _____

8. Which two garments should not be put in the dryer?

   _____

9. Which two garments are made of only one type of fabric?

   _____

10. Which label tells you not to use bleach?

   _____

 Write About It!

Read the washing instructions for one of your own garments such as a shirt, pants, or jacket. Explain how the garment should be cleaned.

Read a Product Warranty

Real-Life Scenario

Andres loves playing his handheld electronic game that he got for his tenth birthday. But when he turned it on this morning, it didn't work. He changed the batteries and tried again. No luck! He couldn't understand how it could be broken already. He'd only gotten it three months ago. His dad told him to find the original box the game came in, and to look for the warranty. He said the warranty would explain if the company would fix it for free or if they would have to pay for it.

What's at Stake
Getting the game fixed.

Teach

Step 1

Set the Stage
- Read aloud the *Real-Life Scenario* and *What's at Stake*.
- Tell students that most products come with a warranty. Explain that a warranty is like a promise from the manufacturer. It's a guarantee that the product will perform correctly or not break within a certain time period. If it does break in that time period, the manufacturer guarantees that it will fix or replace the product. The purpose of a warranty is to protect the consumer.
- Encourage students to share personal stories about products they have owned that have broken. Ask them if they were able to replace it or get it fixed using the warranty.

Step 2

Overview
- Review the vocabulary in the *Words to Know* box.
- Point out that warranties are usually written in fine print. Explain the term *fine print*. Emphasize to students that just because the print is small does not mean that it is not important. The *fine print* is often very important information!
- Read through the *Product Warranty* with students.
- Ask students to summarize in their own words what this warranty says.

Step 3

Guided Questions
These are suggested questions to ask your students. Read them aloud.

❶ For how long is the warranty for this product?

❷ Suppose Andres's game fell in the pool by mistake and now it's not working. Is it covered by the warranty?

❸ Let's say Andres has no idea why his game isn't working. As far as he knows, he didn't cause it to break in any way. Is it covered by the warranty?

❹ Why does Andres need to include a check for $7 if he mails back his game?

❺ Besides the defective game, what other things does Andres need to put in the box before he ships it back to the manufacturer?

Have students complete the *Vocabulary Quick Check.*

Step 4

Discuss the *Think About It!* question about lifetime warranties, and the *Be Smart!* tip about extended warranties.

Step 5

Now It's Your Turn
Have students work individually or with a partner to complete the *Now It's Your Turn* page.

Name _____ Date _____

Read a Product Warranty

LIMITED ONE-YEAR WARRANTY

Gametime, Inc. warrants this product to be free of **defects** in workmanship and materials, under normal use, for a period of one year from the date of original purchase.

NOTE: OUR WARRANTY DOES NOT APPLY TO ANY PRODUCT THAT HAS BEEN DAMAGED BY NEGLIGENCE, MISUSE, OR ACCIDENT. THE WARRANTY WILL BECOME VOID IF THE DAMAGE TO THE PRODUCT IS DUE TO THE OWNER'S NEGLIGENCE.

If service is required during the warranty period, **Gametime, Inc.** will repair or replace the product without charge (except for a $7.00 charge for handling and return postage).

Return the product to the Factory Service Center listed below, with your sales receipt. Circle the date of purchase on the receipt.

Before returning the item:
1. Remove the batteries and pack the item in a sturdy box.
2. Enclose your sales receipt. Circle the purchase date.
3. Enclose a check or money order for the sum of $7.00.

Send the unit to:
Consumer Repair Department
Gametime, Inc.
7890 Silver Drive
Oakville, CA 70548

Words to Know

defects—problems or imperfections

enclose—include

handling—the transportation and packaging of goods

malfunctioned—didn't perform or work properly

negligence—carelessness

warranty—a guarantee

unit—item

workmanship—the product of a worker

void—cancelled

 Think About It!

Why do you think companies usually give customers limited warranties and not lifetime warranties?

Be Smart!

Electronic items are not always reliable. Sometimes stores sell extended warranties. An extended warranty guarantees that the product can be fixed even if the time limit of the original warranty expires. Depending on the price, an extended warranty can be a smart purchase.

Vocabulary Quick Check
Choose the right answer.

1. **Negligence** is
   a. getting the game wet by mistake
   b. not turning the game off when finished playing

2. According to a manufacturer, a **defect** would be
   a. a part that you broke
   b. a part that came broken

3. A **warranty** is a
   a. form of protection for the consumer
   b. an order form

Name _____ Date _____

Read a Product Warranty

Step 1
Read the bicycle warranty.

LIMITED WARRANTY for Sprint Bicycles Models #7530 and #7540
THE LIMITED WARRANTY IS VALID FOR THE ORIGINAL CONSUMER ONLY.

What does the Limited Warranty cover?
The Limited Warranty covers all parts of the bicycle.

What is not covered by the warranty?
• normal wear and tear
• damage due to improper assembly, use, or storage

The warranty will be void if at any time the bicycle is:
• used in a competitive sport, or for stunt riding or jumping
• ridden by more than one person at a time
• transferred, rented, or sold to another person

Length of the Limited Warranty
Bicycle parts are warranted for one year from the date of purchase.
The bicycle frame is warranted for life.

How to Use the Warranty
Sprint Bicycles will replace any defective part. The original owner must pay for all shipping charges. Contact the Customer Service Department at 1-800-252-0011.

Step 2 **Answer these questions.**

1. For how long does the warranty cover problems with bicycle parts?

_____

2. What part of the bike has a lifetime warranty?

_____

3. What would be an example of normal wear and tear on a bicycle?

_____

4. Name three things that would make the warranty void?

_____

_____

5. Why do you think the manufacturer doesn't guarantee the bike if it is used for stunt riding?

_____

6. If you need to use the warranty, what will Sprint pay for? What must the customer pay for?

_____

7. Suppose the bike is nine months old. You have outgrown it and sold it to your neighbor. Can the neighbor use the warranty if something breaks? Explain why.

_____

_____

Write About It!
Imagine that you are Andres. On another piece of paper, write a letter to the manufacturer explaining why you need warranty service.

Building Real-Life Reading Skills • © 2009 by Cindy Harris • Scholastic Teaching Resources

Answer Key

Pages 7–9
Read a Sign for Store Hours

Guided Questions

1. Latoya and her father can return on Tuesday since the store is open until 9:30 p.m.
2. Friday has the longest store hours. The story is open from 9:30 a.m. to 10:00 p.m.
3. Saturday has the shortest store hours.
4. The store opens at 9:30 a.m. on most days of the week.
5. Monday and Wednesday have identical store hours.

Vocabulary Quick Check

1. p.m.
2. p.m.
3. p.m.

Think About It!
Friday night and Saturday night are part of the weekend, when people usually have off from work. More people shop during these times so the stores stay open later hoping to bring in more sales.

Now It's Your Turn

1. 11:00 p.m.
2. Yes. The Allwood Street location opens early at 7 a.m.
3. Neither location is open until midnight.
4. The Colfax Avenue location is open the latest on Mondays and Tuesdays.
5. The Allwood Street location opens the earliest most days of the week.
6. The Colfax Avenue location stays open the latest on most nights.
7. The Colfax Avenue location has longer hours on Sunday.
8. You could contact the store by calling on the phone or emailing the store.

Write About It! Sign designs will vary, but should reflect 10 a.m.–5 p.m. hours Monday through Saturday; closed on Sunday.

Pages 10–12
Read an Invitation & Directions

Guided Questions

1. Ten years old.
2. The party is on Friday, May 3rd at 4:30.
3. The party will take place at Miguel's home at 65 Ridge Road.
4. No. The Martinez's only want to hear from people who can't come to the party. It says Regrets Only.
5. If Carlos can't go, he should email to let them know.
6. He should walk out the school driveway and make a right.

7. He should walk two blocks and turn left onto Ridge Road.
8. The directions repeat the street number and mention that the house is blue and that it is on the corner.

Vocabulary Quick Check

1. block
2. head
3. RSVP

Think About It!
When people send an invitation that says RSVP Regrets Only, they don't want to hear back from everyone they invite. They only want to know who can't come and assume that everyone else will show up.

Now It's Your Turn

1. The cookout is at Memorial Park on Tuesday, June 5th, from 4:00 to 6:00 p.m.
2. The cookout is for two hours.
3. The cookout costs $5.
4. They should tell the scout master, John Conner, if they can attend.
5. They should notify him by email.
6. The starting point for the directions is the school.
7. They should head north.
8. At Independence Way, the scouts should make a left.
9. The road that leads into the park is Memorial Drive.
10. They will meet at Memorial Statue at 4:00 p.m.

Write About It! Answers will vary.

Pages 13–15
Read a Recipe

Guided Questions

1. The first step in the recipe is to preheat the oven to 350 degrees.
2. A greased pan is a pan with oil or fat on it, which prevents the batter from sticking to the pan while it is baking. You can use Crisco or non-stick spray to grease a pan.
3. You need to use a large bowl so that you can mix all of the ingredients together, like the recipe says. If the bowl is too small, it will overflow and all the ingredients won't be together.
4. To fold chocolate chips into the batter if you want to, you would put chocolate chips in the batter and stir the two together with large, slow strokes.
5. You should bake the brownies for 35 to 45 minutes.
6. A pan that is 8 x 8 is 8 inches long and 8 inches wide; a 9 x 9 pan is 9 inches long and 9 inches wide.
7. You can determine whether to cook the brownies for 35 or 45 minutes by looking at them after 35 minutes and testing them to see if they are done.

8. To decorate the brownies, the recipe suggests that you use a strawberry, or sprinkle them with confectioners' sugar.
9. If Emma sells the all brownies for $.50 and the recipe makes 20 brownies, she will make $10.00.

Vocabulary Quick Check

1. b. to flavor
2. a. lightly mix together
3. b. a tiny bit

Think About It!
If you do not cook brownies long enough, they will be mushy and can make you sick. If you cook them for too long, they will burn.

Now It's Your Turn

1. You must have the English muffin, the tomato sauce, and the cheese.
2. The optional ingredients are the toppings such as onion, broccoli, or mushrooms and the seasonings such as oregano, garlic powder, and red pepper flakes.
3. The first step is to preheat the toaster oven or oven.
4. After spreading the sauce, you should sprinkle cheese on top.
5. The two steps that require adult assistance are preheating the oven and removing the pizza from the oven because these are dangerous for children to do alone.
6. If the cheese is hot and bubbly and the pizza has only been cooking for 6 minutes, it is ready and you should take it out of the oven.
7. If you don't have English muffins, you can use bagels or pita bread.
8. A tool you can use to make sure that you cook food for the right amount of time is a kitchen timer.
9. This recipe serves 1 person.
10. After you take the pizza out of the oven but before you eat it, you need to let it cool so it does not burn your mouth.

Write About It! Answers will vary.

Pages 16–18
Read a Check

Guided Questions

1. This check is worth $25.00. You can look on the line where the amount is written as a number, or below it, where it is written out in words.
2. You can find the person's name who is writing the check in the upper left corner and on the signature line.
3. The memo line is for writing a short note. The note on the memo line of this check says "Congratulations."
4. The date is June 22, 2010.
5. The line after the words "Pay to the order of" is the line that has the

name of the person to whom the check is made out.

Vocabulary Quick Check

1. endorse
2. payor
3. memo line

Think About It!
The person writing the check has to sign the check so that the bank can verify the person's signature if need be. Signing the check prevents people from stealing checks and using them.

Now It's Your Turn

1. Line C
2. Line G
3. Line I
4. Line D
5. Line H
6. Line B
7. Line A
8. Line E

Write About It! Answers will vary.

Pages 19–21
Read a Restaurant Menu

Guided Questions

1. This restaurant serves French cuisine.
2. Dinner is served starting at 4 p.m.
3. You would ask the waiter or waitress.
4. Salad and house dressing is served with each entrée or main course.
5. You would get a bigger portion of food with an entrée because an entrée is a main course while hors d'oeuvres are starter courses or appetizers. These are always smaller portions.
6. A la carte items do not come with the main course. They are ordered separately.
7. Answers will vary.
8. The tip is automatically added to the bill.

Vocabulary Quick Check

1. False. Soup du jour is the soup of the day.
2. False. The customer gives the waiter a tip or gratuity.
3. True. Hors d'oeuvres, starters, and appetizers are synonyms.

Think About It!
Possible responses:
- I think it is right that some restaurants include the tip for the waiter on the bill because a lot of people do not tip their waiters enough, and waiters work very hard to make sure that the customers enjoy their meal. Many cultures also do not tip their waiters, and if people from different cultures go out to eat here and don't know about tipping, the waiters sometimes are not paid for their hard work.
- I think it is wrong that some restaurants include the tip for the waiter on the bill because the tip should be the customer's decision. If a waiter does not do a good job, a customer can then decide if, or how much, to tip him.

Now It's Your Turn
1. Salads are Starters.
2. House Salad is served with every dinner.
3. French Fries cost $3.50.
4. Vegetarian Chili, Personal Pizza, and Lasagna.
5. The Rib Eye Steak is the most expensive entrée.
6. No. It is not a choice on the menu.
7. You cannot switch because the menu states, "no substitutions."
8. The tip will not be added to the bill because it is only added if there are 6 or more people eating together.

Write About It! Answers will vary.

Pages 22–24
Read a Sports Schedule

Guided Questions
1. Game 3 is Away
2. There are 10 games in all. Five are at home. Five are away.
3. The Tigers play the Wolves on Thursday, April 2nd at 5:30.
4. The games begin in March and end in May.
5. Game #6 starts at 5:00 p.m.
6. Most games are in the afternoon.
7. They play the Blue Jays and the Cardinals twice.
8. Most games are played on Tuesdays, Thursdays, and Saturdays.

Vocabulary Quick Check
1. False. A home game is played on your team's field.
2. True. An opponent competes against your team.
3. False. A division is made up of teams, not seasons.

Think About It!
Answers will vary. Here is a possible response:
Anthony can use a pen or marker to cross out the games he already played. He could use a highlighter to highlight the upcoming games.

Now It's Your Turn
1. The Sharks and the Wolves
2. There are five opponents in all.
3. The games take place on Mondays and Wednesdays.
4. They play during the months of May and June.
5. They'll play four games at Home.
6. The earliest the games begin is at 4:00 p.m. The latest they begin is at 5:30 p.m.
7. The wolves play on Wednesdays. But they play their last game against the Sharks on a Monday.
8. They'll play two Away games.
9. The Sharks and the Wolves will play against each other in the last game.
10. The teams will play at home.

Write About It! Answers will vary.

Pages 25–27
Read a Lobby Directory

Guided Questions
1. It is arranged in order by level and by suite.
2. There are three floors.
3. There are 11 offices.
4. His office is on Level 2 (the second floor) in Suite 201. The name of his practice is Family Eye Center.
5. Dr. Gonzales is an allergist.
6. Those offices are not occupied.
7. You would be able to figure out where to go if you looked for a dental practice on the directory. Since there is only one dental practice listed, you could assume that Dr. Kane is part of the Tustin Dental Office.

Vocabulary Quick Check
1. directory
2. suite
3. lobby

Think About It!
Answers will vary. Students might say they would make the directory in alphabetical order because that makes it easy to look up names.

Now It's Your Turn
1. It is arranged first by floor and then in alphabetical order on that floor.
2. There are two floors. There are 13 rooms in all.
3. You would go to Room 209, the Recreation office.
4. You would go to Room 200 for the Senior Citizens Program.
5. They probably need a marriage license.
6. You would go to Police in Room 102 to report a crime.
7. You would go to the Health Clinic in Room 204 for a vaccination.
8. Answers will vary.

Write About It! Answers will vary.

Pages 28–30
Read Instant-Food Directions

Guided Questions
1. Remove the plastic wrap that covers the bag.
2. You should put the microwave bag in the microwave with the instructions side of the bag facing up.
3. The suggested time is 2 to 5 minutes.
4. Open the bag by pulling diagonally on the bag's opposite corners.
5. The popcorn will burn.
6. No. The warning says not to reheat the unpopped kernels.
7. There are two helpful hints. One hint says to shake the bag before you open it so the flavoring gets all over the popcorn. Another hint says not to turn off the microwave and then start it again while you are microwaving the popcorn.

Vocabulary Quick Check
1. instant
2. optimum
3. steam

Now It's Your Turn
1. Take off the paper overwrap.
2. Peel it halfway.
3. up to the line on the inside of the cup
4. Close the lid.
5. Wait 3 minutes.
6. It is necessary to stir well so the flavors get mixed in well.
7. The soup ingredients probably wouldn't be cooked yet.
8. The soup would be cold.

Write About It! Answers will vary.

Pages 31–33
Read Parking Signs

Guided Questions
1. You can park here any day of the week except on Tuesday and Thursdays from 7 a.m. until 6 p.m.
2. This space is a bus stop. No parking is allowed.
3. Yes. Parking is permitted on Sundays.
4. Yes, because on Sunday a permit isn't required.
5. He can never park the car next to sign #2 – the bus stop.
6. The arrows show in which direction, from the place where sign is posted, a person can or can't park.

Vocabulary Quick Check
1. a. section
2. b. certificate
3. a. time

Think About It!
If a sign says that No Standing is allowed, then parking the car there is not allowed either. If you are not allowed to park there and wait in the car, then you are also not allowed to park there and leave the car there for an extended period of time.

Now It's Your Turn
1. You can park there all the time with a permit. You can park there without a permit before 9 a.m. and after 5 p.m.
2. You need a permit.
3. sign #3
4. sign #2, #4, and #5 (unless the road is covered with snow)
5. You can park there before noon or after 8 p.m., or any time on Sunday.
6. You must put money in the meter.
7. Sample answers: On Monday at 7:30 p.m. and on Wednesday at 6:00 a.m.
8. Sign #5 is related to weather conditions.
9. The purpose of this sign is to allow the snow plows to clear the road.

Write About It! Answers will vary.

Pages 34–36
Read an Amusement Park Operation & Rates Schedule

Guided Questions
1. The regular admissions price for ages 7 to 59 is $25.00.
2. It will cost 5-year-old Kim Schmidt $17.00 to spend the day at the amusement park.
3. Grandpa needs to be 60 years old to pay the senior citizen price.
4. All of July and all of August, except the 30th and 31st.
5. The last week of August, the park is open until 7 p.m.
6. The park is closed weekdays in September because school has started and no kids are going to be coming to the park with their families.
7. The park offers a Preview Plan.
8. The Preview Plan lets the family go to the park two days in a row. They pay for a regular admission ticket 3 hours before the park closes one day, and then go again to the park the next day without paying again.

Vocabulary Quick Check
1. No. The third, fourth, and sixth days of July are not consecutive days.
2. Yes. Breakfast is prior to lunch.
3. No. You do not pay admission when you leave the park.

Think About It!
If a family plans on going to the amusement park many times throughout the summer, they should buy season tickets because it is cheaper than buying regular admission tickets every time they go to the park. If someone only wants to go to the park once or twice though, it is not reasonable to buy the season tickets.

Now It's Your Turn
1. The water park is closed on July 29th and August 31st.
2. On the weekends, the park is open until 10 p.m.
3. On weekdays, the park opens at 11 a.m.
4. On July 4th the water park is open from 9 a.m. until 10 p.m.
5. It costs $20 for an adult to go to the park on a Thursday.
6. It is cheaper to go to the park on weekdays.
7. On Independence Day, a child pays $20 to get into the park.
8. No. There is not a senior citizen discount for the water park.
9. It would cost $15 for a 5 year old to go to the park on a Tuesday.
10. If you go to the water park on 3 different weekends, you should buy a season pass because $75 is cheaper than $84. If you go on

weekdays, you should buy three separate admission tickets because $60 is cheaper than $75.

Write About It! Answers will vary.

Pages 37–39
Read a Magazine Subscription Form

Guided Questions
1. A one-year subscription now is $19.
2. The regular price for a one-year subscription is $25.
3. A subscriber will save $6 on a one-year subscription by ordering via the subscription form.
4. A two-year subscription is $36.
5. If Jeremy orders a one-year subscription, he will get 12 issues.
6. You cannot get the free minibook of puzzles if you already get the magazine because it is a special offer only for new subscribers.
7. The postage will be paid by the addressee, the magazine subscription company.

Vocabulary Quick Check
1. False. Annual means yearly.
2. False. The addressee is the person receiving the postcard.
3. True. An issue is a single copy.

Think About It!
The advantage is that you can save money if you know that you will want the magazine for two years.

Now It's Your Turn
1. A one-year subscription is $12.50.
2. A two-year subscription is $21.00.
3. A two-year subscription is a better deal because you get 22 issues for $21.00 instead of $25.00.
4. There are 11 issues in an annual subscription.
5. An issue of the magazine will not come in the month of August.
6. No. You would only receive a gift if you ordered a subscription.
7. To receive a compass and the surprise gifts, you must order a two-year subscription.
8. Jeremy must not pay any money to mail the subscription form because it is already post marked by *Science for Kids.*
9. The magazine guarantees its readers the compass and the two other surprise gifts throughout the year, plus satisfaction with the magazine. If a reader is not satisfied, they may call and cancel their subscription at any time.
10. No. You do not have to pay in advance. The magazine will bill you later.

Write About It! Answers will vary.

Pages 40–42
Read a Skin-Care Product Label

Guided Questions
1. Meg needs to apply sunscreen after swimming. It says reapply after 60 minutes of swimming.
2. If she plays Frisbee for 20 minutes she does not need to reapply sunscreen.
3. If she is in the water for two hours, she does need to reapply sunscreen.
4. If the sunscreen gets in her eyes, Meg should rinse her eyes with water.
5. If she gets a rash from the sunscreen, Meg should not continue to use that particular sunscreen and find another one that will not irritate her skin. She could also wear a hat and long sleeve clothing to protect her skin.
6. To apply sunscreen liberally means that Meg should use a lot of sunscreen all over her entire body, making sure every part of her skin is protected.
7. Perspiration causes sunscreen to wear off faster than water.

Vocabulary Quick Check
1. external
2. exposed
3. maximum

Think About It!
Sample Answers:
- I am very fair skinned, with light-colored hair and eyes. Therefore, I burn very easily and need to apply SPF 30 or 45 multiple times throughout the day. I also try to wear a hat and long clothing to cover myself from the sun.
- I have medium-toned skin, with dark hair and dark eyes. My skin sometimes gets sunburned, but not as easily as other people. I still wear SPF 25 or 30 to protect myself and I apply it regularly, but if I forget a hat I won't get badly burnt.
- I have darker skin and dark hair and eyes. Because I am so dark, many people think I can't get sunburned but that is not true. When I go to the beach or the pool or play outside for a long time, I wear SPF 10 or 15. Sometimes if I am going to be out all day, I wear SPF 25. I wear hats because I like them, not because I need them to protect my head and face from the sun.

Now It's Your Turn
1. Bugs Away! will keep insects away for up to 2 hours.
2. Bugs Away! keeps away mosquitoes, ticks, gnats, and chiggers. (Answers should include two of these insects.)

3. The spray bottle should be held 8 inches away from your skin before spraying.
4. To apply Bugs Away! to your face, you should spray it into your hand first and then rub it on to your face without putting it near the eyes or mouth.
5. In the Warning section, the word "irritation" means "discomfort."
6. Young children should not use Bugs Away! without supervision because it is a chemical product and can be dangerous for them if they get it in their eyes or mouth. Children also have sensitive skin, and it could irritate their skin.

Write About It! Answers will vary.

Pages 43–45
Read a Nutrition Facts Label

Guided Questions
1. The nacho cheese tortilla chips have more calories per serving.
2. The nacho cheese tortilla chips have more cholesterol per serving.
3. There are about 10 chips in one serving of nachos. There are 32 pretzels in one serving of pretzels.
4. The pretzels have 0 grams of fat, less than the chips, which have 11 grams of fat.
5. The nacho chips have 2 grams of fiber, more fiber than the pretzels.

Vocabulary Quick Check
1. calories
2. cholesterol
3. sodium

Think About It!
No. Dr. Kramer would not approve of Jake's choice to eat tortilla chips because the chips have a lot of fat in them (11 grams per serving) and are much higher in cholesterol than the pretzels (19 grams versus 0 grams). Even though pretzels are high in sodium, they are a healthier choice than the chips.

Now It's Your Turn
1. 8 fluid ounces is one serving of milk.
2. There are two servings per container.
3. Whole milk has more calories.
4. Whole milk has 8 grams of fat. Skim milk has 0 grams of fat.
5. There are 5 grams of saturated fat in a serving of whole milk. There are 0 grams of saturated fat in a serving of skim milk.
6. Whole milk has more cholesterol.
7. c. The Vitamin C and Vitamin A content are different.
8. There are 8 grams of protein in a cup of milk.
9. A cup of milk gives you 30% of your daily calcium needs.

10. Skim milk has more Vitamin A.

Write About It! Answers will vary.

Pages 46–48
Read Merchandise Tags

Guided Questions
1. The size is XL or size 14/16.
2. The price is $6.99.
3. This shirt was made in China.
4. These pants are blue.
5. The size is a medium. The price is $14.99.
6. The style number is 9875.
7. The brand is KIDCITY.

Vocabulary Quick Check
XS = extra small
M = medium
XXL = extra, extra large
12S = size 12 slim
14H = size 14 husky

Think About It!
One Size Fits All means that the item only comes in one size and it fits most people.

Now It's Your Turn
1. size 10/12
2. sky blue
3. It is a coat.
4. $25.00
5. COATSforYOU.com
6. medium or size 8
7. red
8. $29.99
9. The store saves you $10.
10. The style number is 2601.

Write About It! Answers will vary.

Pages 49–51
Read an Ingredients List

Guided Questions
1. The second most abundant ingredient in this type of cereal bar is tapioca starch.
2. These cereal bars contain more sugar. You know because sugar is listed before oil on the ingredients list.
3. There are 18 ingredients in this cereal bar.
4. This is not a food Tyron can eat because it may contain traces of peanuts. It was made on equipment that processes foods made with peanuts and peanut derivatives.
5. It means the oil in this food is either canola oil or soybean oil, or both.

Vocabulary Quick Check
1. a. bits
2. b. man-made
3. b. added

Think About It!
It is important to read the items in parentheses because these usually show the combination of

the ingredient listed right before the parentheses. This may tell you important information for people who are allergic to certain foods.

To find out what natural flavors are in the cereal bar, you could look for ingredients that are grown on the earth and not processed before being put into the cereal bar. You can also call the cereal bar company and ask them questions about the natural ingredients in their products.

Now It's Your Turn

1. The main ingredient in this cracker is enriched wheat flour.
2. The sub-ingredients in this ingredient are wheat flour, niacin, reduced iron, thiamin mononitrate, riboflavin, and folic acid.
3. If a person is allergic to soy it is not safe to eat this product because the partially hydrogenated vegetable oil contains soybean oil, and there's also soy lecithin in the crackers.
4. A person who is allergic to peanuts can eat this cracker because peanuts are not on the ingredient list and it was not made in an area where peanuts are processed.
5. Wheat flour can be enriched with niacin, iron, thiamin, riboflavin, mononitrate, and folic acid.
6. This cracker contains 2% or less of: (Answers will vary. See Ingredients List, page 51.)
7. Certain ingredients are listed in bold type because they are important ingredients to notice if someone who is allergic to wheat, soybean oil, or soy is considering eating this product.

Write About It! Answers will vary.

Pages 52–54
Read a Toy-Store Flyer

Guided Questions

1. She must purchase a bicycle worth $99 or more. It is really worth $19.99.
2. She must buy 2 or more cartridges.
3. The words "in store only" mean that this offer is only good if you buy the items in the store, as opposed to buying by the items through a mail-order catalog or online.
4. No. This scooter is a Toy World exclusive, which means it is not sold in other stores.
5. It will cost $24.99 when Isabel goes to pay for it, but after she sends in the rebate, and gets $5 back in the mail, it will have cost only $19.99.

Vocabulary Quick Check

1. Fine print is small print.
2. A rebate is money that you will be refunded.

3. A rain check is a type of guarantee that says you will get the product at a later date for the sale price.

Think About It!
If a store says that they have only limited quantities, they are telling the customer that they do not have a lot of that product and if you really want to buy it, you need to come to the store or order from the catalog very quickly, before the store runs out of the product.

Now It's Your Turn

1. The sale price is $39.99.
2. The original price was $49.99.
3. Tic Tac Toe, Marbles, Checkers, Chess, and Bingo are the Buy 1 Get 1 Free games.
4. No substitutions means that another game cannot be substituted for one of those listed.
5. Each store may not have the same selection because the advertisement says "Selection may vary by store."
6. At the store, you will have to pay $19.99 for the movie.
7. You will get $10 back in the mail after sending in the rebate.
8. The sale is going on from January 5th until January 13th.

Write About It! Answers will vary.

Pages 55–57
Read Clothing-Care Labels

Guided Questions

1. cold water
2. colors
3. It would be necessary if the shirt is wrinkled after it comes out of the dryer.
4. wool
5. It means that you should not do that action to the garment.

Vocabulary Quick Check

1. False. It removes color.
2. False. Dry cleaning uses chemicals.
3. True. It can go in the dryer.

Think About It!
Warmer temperatures remove dirt best, but may also remove some of the colored dyes. That is why it is best to wash whites in hot water, so that the dirt will be released from the fabric. On the other hand, colored clothes wash best in cooler water. This keeps the dyes in the fabric while still getting out the dirt.

Now It's Your Turn

1. cotton
2. You might use bleach if the garment is white and has stains.
3. It should be washed in cold water.
4. It means "DO NOT" wash/clean/dry, etc. in this way.
5. It should be hung up to dry.
6. silk

7. dry clean
8. garment #2 and garment #3
9. garment #1 and garment #3
10. garment #2

Write About It! Answers will vary.

Pages 58–60
Read a Product Warranty

Guided Questions

1. The warranty for this product is one year from the date of original purchase.
2. If Andres's game got wet and broke when it fell in the pool by accident, it is not covered by warranty because the warranty does not apply to any product that has been damaged by accident or negligence.
3. If Andres has no idea why the game is not working and did not do anything to break the game, it is covered by warranty because Gametime, Inc. guarantees that the product will be free of defects in workmanship and materials with normal use.
4. He needs to include a $7 check if he mails back the game to cover the costs of handling and return postage.
5. Along with the defective game, Andres should remove the batteries from the game and put it in a sturdy box. He should also include the sales receipt, with the purchase date circled, and the check for $7.

Vocabulary Quick Check

1. a. getting the game wet by mistake
2. b. a part that came broken
3. a. form of protection for the consumer

Think About It!
Companies give customers limited warranties instead of lifetime warranties because over the course of time and with a lot of use, a product will most likely break or stop working. By giving everyone a lifetime warranty, the company will end up replacing all the old and broken products for free. Instead, when an old product breaks, the company wants the customer to buy a new product.

Now It's Your Turn

1. The warranty covers problems with bicycle parts for one year from the date of purchase of the bicycle.
2. The frame of the bicycle has a lifetime warranty.
3. An example of normal wear and tear on a bicycle would be if the seat gets worn or faded.
4. Three things that would make the warranty void are if the bicycle breaks while being used in

a competitive sport, stunt riding or jumping, if it is ridden by more than one person at a time, and if it is transferred, rented, or sold to another person.
5. The manufacturer doesn't guarantee the bike if it is used for stunt riding because doing stunts is rough on a bicycle and will cause it to break easily. The company does not want to give people a warranty if they ride the bicycle irresponsibly.
6. If you need to use the warranty, Sprint will pay for the defective parts of the bicycle, but the customer must pay for all the shipping charges.
7. The neighbor cannot use the warranty if a part of the bike breaks because the warranty does not apply to the bike anymore once it is rented, sold, or transferred to another person.

Write About It! Answers will vary.